AF529477

Crusader or Conspirator?

Coalgate and Other Truths

Attention Authors

'We Convert Fighters into Writers'. That's the motto of Manas Publications since more than four decades. Our message to the world is that India can win the battle not only by the bullet but also by the pen. There is no dearth of intellectuals in our country, but their knowledge is confined to them only. No sincere effort has been made by any other publisher to channelise their knowledge in national interest. That is why the talent of a large number of intellectuals remains latent. An author transforms his knowledge into a manuscript, and it is our job to spread his/her knowledge by converting it into a beautiful book. For over four decades, Manas has been motivating the intellectuals by publishing their manuscripts and would like to publish your manuscript too. If you or your colleagues have any manuscript ready for publication or are working on it, kindly contact us with detailed synopsis and list of contents. We will transform your work into a valuable publication. If you wish, we can also suggest you the suitable subjects for writing the books related to your area of expertise. Manas is known for its publishing quality and commitments. We take utmost care in production and give wide publicity to the book as well as its author through our national and international distribution network.

CRUSADER *or* CONSPIRATOR?

Coalgate and Other Truths

PC Parakh, IAS (Retd)
Former Secretary, Ministry of Coal

Manas Publications
(We Convert Fighters into Writers)
New Delhi-110002 (INDIA)

MANAS PUBLICATIONS
(We Convert Fighters into Writers)
(Publishers, Library Suppliers, Importers & Exporters)
4402/5-A, Ansari Road (Opp. HDFC Bank)
Darya Ganj, New Delhi-110 002 (India)
Off: ✆ 011-23260783, 23265523, Res: 011-23842660
Fax: 011-23272766
E-mail: manaspublications@gmail.com
manaspublications@yahoo.com
Website: www.manaspublications.in

© PC Parakh
2014

Royalty on this will be shared between the Transparency International and the Arihant Charitable Trust.

ISBN: 978-81-7049-487-4
₹ 595/-

All rights reserved. This book is sold subject to the condition that it shall not, by way of trade or otherwise, be lent, resold, hired out, or otherwise circulated, without the publisher's prior written consent, in any form of binding, soft cover or e-version etc., except by the authorised companies and without a similar condition including this condition being imposed on the subsequent purchaser and without limiting the rights under copyright reserved above, no part of this publication may be reproduced, stored in or introduced into a retrieval system, or transmitted in any form or by any means (electrical, mechanical, photocopying, recording or otherwise) without prior written permission of the publisher of the book.

Cataloguing/listing of this book for re-sale purpose can be done, only by the authorised companies. Cataloguing/listing or sale by unauthorised distributors/ bookshops/booksellers etc is strictly prohibited and will be legally prosecuted.

The views expressed in this book are those of the author and not at all of the publisher. The publisher is not responsible for the views of the author or anybody as well as authenticity of the data/ text, in any way whatsoever.

All disputes are subject to Delhi jurisdiction only.

Designed at
Manas Publications

Printed in India at
RK Print Services, Delhi
and published by Mrs Suman Lata for
Manas Publications, 4402/5-A,
Ansari Road, (Opp HDFC Bank),
Darya Ganj, New Delhi-110 002 (INDIA)

To my mother late Chand Kunwar who instilled a strong commitment to honesty and impartiality and to my wife Usha and daughter Sushmita who never made demands that could not be met out of my modest salary as a civil servant and who stood by me in the thick and thin of life.

"An efficient, disciplined and contented service, assured of its prospects as a result of diligent and honest work, is *sine qua non* of sound administration under a democratic regime even more than under authoritarian rule. The service must be above party and we should ensure that political considerations, either in its recruitment or in its discipline, are reduced to the minimum, if not eliminated altogether."

—Sardar Vallabhbhai Patel
First Deputy Prime Minister and
first Home Minister of India

Contents

Part Two

MINISTRY OF COAL

Part Three

CODE FOR THE FUTURE

List of Annexures

10. **Annexure 10-II:** Extracts from the report of the House Committee of the Andhra Pradesh Legislature that enquired Into the Irregularities by the Private Management of Nizam Sugars Limited, 31st of August 2006
11. **Annexure 14-I:** Note dated 17.01.2005 submitted to the PMO requesting intervention to expedite approval of Cabinet Note for introducing competitive bidding for allocation of coal blocks
12. **Annexure 17-I:** Note dated 18.02.2005 of MoS seeking my explanation for referring Mr Shashi Kumar's appointment to ACC, though the Minister had rejected his name
13. **Annexure 18-I:** Letter No. CMD:ES:F-19:04: 604 dated 06.12.2004 from the CMD, BCCL about activities of Mr CS Dubey MP, hampering operations of BCCL
14. **Annexure 18-II:** Letter dated 08.11.2004 from Mr CS Dubey MP addressed to the Prime Minister seeking investigations by CVC or a Parliamentary Committee for my misconduct
15. **Annexure 18-III:** My letter No. Secy@/11019/04 dated: 06.12.04 addressed to the Cabinet Secretary in response to Mr Dubey's complaint to the Prime Minister
16. **Annexure 18-IV:** My letter No. 7192/Secy (Coal) dated 21.06.2005 addressed to the Cabinet Secretary seeking action against Mr Narendra Kumar Kushwaha MP for blackmailing Mr VK Singh, CMD, NCL
17. **Annexure 18-V:** Letter No. CVC/2005/87/1349 dated 08.07.2005 from Mr P Shankar CVC suggesting course of action to deal with problem of blackmail by MPs

18. **Annexure 18-VI:** My letter No. Secy(Coal)/8.8.05 dated 18.08.2005 addressed to the Cabinet Secretary seeking a meeting of the Committee of Secretaries to discuss problem of blackmail by MPs

19. **Annexure 18-VII:** Letter No. 600(AC)/31/C/28-(417)/05-ES.II dated 02.08.2005 from Ms V Vidyavathi, Director, PMO informing that allegations made by Mr Furkan Ansari and Mr CS Dubey MPs against Mr RP Retolia CMD, CCL were found to be false

20. **Annexure 18-VIII:** Letter No. CIL: CONF/584 Dated 19.11.2005 from Mr Shashi Kumar CMD, CIL informing use of abusive and threatening language by Mr Ananth Kumar Chairman of the standing committee of Parliament

21. **Annexure 18-IX:** My note dated 30.11.2005 to the MoS informing about misconduct of Mr Ananth Kumar and take such action as he and PM consider appropriate

22. **Annexure 18-X:** My letter No. Secy (Coal)/8.8.05 dated 08.08.2005 addressed to the Cabinet Secretary seeking voluntary retirement following use of abusing language by Mr Dharmendra Pradhan at the consultative Committee of the Parliament

23. **Annexure 18-XI:** My letter No. Secy (Coal) 22.8.05 dated 22.08.2005 addressed to the Cabinet Secretary intimating resumption of duty following meeting with the Prime Minister

24. **Annexure 18-XII:** Letter No. MP(LS)/DGH/05 dated 28.08.2005 from Mr Dharmendra Pradhan MP addressed to the Prime Minister justifying his misconduct at the Parliamentary Standing Committee meeting

25. **Annexure 18-XIII:** Office Memo No. 5401214/2005-CA-II dated 21.10.2005 from the Ministry of Coal addressed to the PMO (Mr KV Pratap Deputy Secretary) in response to letter of Mr Dharmendra Pradhan
26. **Annexure 19-I:** Letter dated 07.02.2004 from Mr Sibu Soren Minister of Coal addressed to the Prime Minister seeking my transfer and action against me for insubordination
27. **Annexure 19-II:** My letter No. 28/S/Secy (Coal) dated 22.03.2005 addressed to the Cabinet Secretary in response to Mr Soren's complaint

Foreword

In our Parliamentary System of governance, the Executive is primarily responsible for providing governance in the country. The System provides for a political executive, which is distinct from the permanent executive. The political executive at the centre and at the state-level is responsible for policy formulation, decision-making in major matters of governance and development, as well as the supervision and monitoring of policy implementation. The bureaucracy mans posts at all levels, from the village to the block, to the district and all the way to the state and Central secretariats; and is primarily responsible for the implementation of tasks handed to it by the political executive and the senior bureaucracy. At its higher levels, the civil service acts as an adviser to the political executive and assists in policy formulation. While wider national policies are, ideally, debated and directed by the party in power, administrative policies are established by the executive. By very nature of things, the work of the political executive and the permanent executive have a large and complex overlap; their smooth and harmonious interaction is an essential prerequisite for good governance.

The bureaucrat and the politician are the two sides of

the governance coin. Their smooth interaction, working in tandem in public interest is the key to good governance. In recent decades it has been noticed that this ideal structure, in practice, has been impaired to a serious extent with the political executive demanding not just servility, but abject obedience to meet the objectives and desires of the former. With a large degree of venality having crept into the political scenario, in effect this means that the minister or political chief demands that the bureaucrat functions in the personal interest of the politician, rather than in public interest. This is the basic cause of the sharp decline in governance standards.

In short, entering politics today is a business venture; much as a young entrepreneur would invest in a business, with the ultimate aim of making a fortune. With honourable exceptions, this has sadly become the rule of the day. Fortunately for the politicians, the courts generally are benign on the grounds of 'privilege of the legislator', and there is no equivalent of a SEBI to watch over malpractices; in short, there is no regulator for politicians—we still await the Lokpal. In the first decades after Independence, much or most of the policy making was proposed, sponsored and developed by officials, especially the higher civil service, finally to obtain the formal approval of the political executive.

By the '70s, the ministers asserted to have their own say on decision-making, especially on individual cases. Policy-making was by and large still left to the bureaucracy; however, the need of the ministers to clear individual cases had become stronger by then. So during the '70s and '80s, it was quite usual for the ministers to overrule their subordinates, and enforce their writ. By the '90s it had become more and more difficult to overrule logical, correct and proper notes in a whimsical way, largely due to adverse attention shown by the courts, as well as the difficulties inherent in attacking a logical well-built case. The need came at that time to transfer out inconvenient secretaries or joint secretaries, and have them replaced with more pliant ones, at least those who would not write so strongly as to make it difficult for the minister to overrule the notings of the secretariat. Generally, the minister would be satisfied to get a wishy-washy note suggesting alternatives including the one that the minister would prefer to approve; clearly he encouraged his officials to firmly indicate the desired course of action, as has been verbally communicated by the minister to the secretary. The above required that the secretariat supporting the minister should be pliant and be willing to co-operate with the minister concerned. They need not really be co-conspirators; it was sufficient if they were intellectually dishonest to write the kind of notes which were really required, and to guide the final decision in the desired manner. Of course there are many variants to this theme, depending on local circumstances and the situation. By and large, the minister wanted a secretary who will 'play ball' with him, even if he was not always required to 'tango' with him. It was the unspoken responsibility of the secretary to the department to handle the lower formations suitably, so that the system functions smoothly. This he did by suitably allocating the work within the department to ensure that he had least difficulty.

Despite all the above, many intrepid secretariat officials, at all levels, would write strong notes supporting or opposing one course of action or the other, irrespective of how the seniors wanted it. Fortunately, even today, there are strong independent officials, having the courage of their convictions and willing to commit their views on paper. However, sadly, a large number of senior officials would not consider continuing with the fight, and would prefer to get sidelined to insignificant areas in the secretariat, where they would not block the mainline traffic, nor be disturbed by the exigencies of the situation.

Parakh's book amply demonstrates, chapter and verse, the sharp deterioration in the standards of the Central Government. The naked venality and corruption that is seen in the districts and in many state secretariats, clearly has reached the Centre. The rot is now fully set in, and is corroding the administrative process. Parakh has correctly noted 'most ills in governance arise due to corruption'. Herein lies the sad explanation as to why seven decades after independence, 70 per cent of the population is in poverty, education standards and health condition of the populace in abysmal condition, and India is an "also ran" among the comity of nations, rather than be seen in the same league, rivalling if not excelling China and USA in world leadership. Parakh has shown a mirror to our system of governance.

Parakh at some stage refers to, self-deprecatingly, "... given my inflexible nature...." Yes, a senior civil servant is expected to be polite, cooperative; however he is not supposed to be intellectually dishonest, or to express views or advice to pander to the personal needs of the politician. Indeed, he is supposed to be 'inflexible' in the positive sense of the term, in that he is ramrod straight—don't forget that he is not the final decision maker in a Parliamentary Democracy—he is only the advisor.

The book also throws light on many aspects of the 'coal scam', which will be of interest to the general public. After all, coal is a mineral, belonging to the public of India—its extraction and distribution is to be done in a fair and open manner, consistent with public interest—not to be conducted through the 'crony capitalism' methodology pursued by the government of the day. To Parakh's credit, he had clearly proposed the auction method, which indeed was approved by the Prime Minister of the day; however, the interests of the politicians involved managed to subvert this sound decision, filibuster its implementation for a decade, while in the mean time ensure that the 'treasury is looted'. The matter is in the highest court.

Suffice it to say that the Prime Minister comes out as a mute, ineffective spectator. Note that the same Prime Minister was able to take a firm stand on the nuclear deal and in FDI in Retail issue; however, he was a wimp in implementing a decision taken by himself, in the face of the corrupt forces surrounding him. Clearly the Prime Minister was a 'prisoner' of circumstances, mostly created by himself. The book also clearly debunks the theory that the CAG's calculation of loss was a spectacular over-assessment; on the contrary, it was very much on the conservative side.

Most insiders, familiar with operations in the Government of India and the State Governments are aware of how CMDs and Directors of public sector corporations are appointed, and how in most such cases the minister concerned and other politicians have a direct personal financial interest. What the book throws light on is only the tip of the iceberg; but the reality is harsh. Equally we have a sample of how the Members of Parliament, who are expected to be policy-makers, but in real life interfere with every element of implementation, almost exclusively for their personal benefit—public interest is nowhere in the picture. The overall fall in administrative standards has been brought out, if anything with some understatement.

The statement by a Minister that we cannot 'put all instructions in writing', with the implication that many things are done by 'mutual understanding' reflects a major malaise in our system. Ministers expect that officials shall obey their verbal orders, without getting them recorded—in other words, the official shall take the responsibility, while the benefit goes to the minister. In this context, it is noteworthy that the Supreme Court recently has found it necessary to step in to stem the rot; the Apex court has invoked the principle of RTI to demand that all official orders should be in writing.

While people like Parakh and Khemka and Durga Nagpal have been in the public eye for having stood up for their principles, the reality is that the system has sharply deteriorated; the political executive will not brook any resistance or 'logic' from the official; the demand that their needs be met instantly is strident.

The coalgate issue is still in the public eye—the court proceedings and collateral activity are still to come. Parakh's book is a timely reminder of the fall in governance standards; and equally an unspoken cry for serious administrative reforms.

New Delhi
April, 2014

TSR Subramanian, IAS (Retd.)
Former Cabinet Secretary
Government of India

Preface

Irrespective of the nature of the State, whether democratic, socialist, capitalist, autocratic or imperialist, the only tool available to it for implementing its policies is its civil service. The efficiency, commitment, honesty and discipline of the civil service will determine the efficacy of its governance.

When India won independence from the British, it inherited the Indian Civil Service (ICS) at the apex of the civil service hierarchy. The ICS was the steel frame on which the entire edifice of the British Empire in India rested. A handful of officers of this service administered the vast Indian Empire with great ability and efficiency. Recruited and trained by a colonial government, although their commitment to democracy and the new political system was a matter of conjecture, there was near unanimity that the members of this service were disciplined, honest and objective.

There were serious differences within the Indian National Congress on the administrative structure of independent India. Jawaharlal Nehru was extremely sceptical of the ICS. He thought the Indian Civil Service was neither Indian nor civil. Nor, he thought, was it about service. Sardar Patel understood and appreciated the value and importance of an honest and independent civil service and the role it would play in building a new nation. As the first home minister of independent India, Patel had tested the ability of the civil service in the unification of the nation and in handling the mammoth post-partition problems of law-and-order and of migrants. Patel's faith in the ability and loyalty of the civil service was unflinching and it was entirely due to his efforts that the Constitution of India provides adequate safeguards to protect civil servants against any capricious action of their political masters.

After independence, not many political leaders shared Patel's vision for the civil service. In the present day, with corruption impacting the entire political system of India, the independence and fearlessness of the civil service as visualised by Patel is considered an affront to the elected political leadership. The differing perceptions of the role of elected representatives and civil servants have totally vitiated the relationship between civil servants and the political executive. This relationship is now either adversarial or collusive. In this situation, many members of the civil service have adapted to the new expectations of the political system. This in turn has seriously undermined the governance of India. The constitutional safeguards, for which Sardar Patel fought single-handedly, have not been able to preserve the integrity, neutrality and independence of the civil service. By a simple and devious tool, the politicians of today's India have undone all that the Sardar worked for. Officers deemed inconvenient, because they are upright, are frequently and arbitrarily transferred or consigned to insignificant assignments. Worse, officers have at times been suspended for offending powerful vested interests in the line of duty. Some have had investigations initiated against them for frivolous reasons.

In this monograph I reflect on and share my experiences while serving with State and Central governments. These are instances that have a bearing on corruption in governance. There are instances of how conflicts arise between civil servants and the political leadership when civil servants are not willing to be party to partisan or wrong decisions. Civil servants invariably suffer when such conflict arises because there is no code of conduct to govern the political class. I too have had moments of agony and frustration because I was forthright and I did not budge from what I thought was right. Yet, I was not victimised or relegated to insignificant assignments. Perhaps the political leadership in Andhra Pradesh was not as vicious and brazen as in other states. Perhaps I had the unflinching support of the Prime Minister, Dr. Manmohan Singh, in the coal ministry. Perhaps I was simply lucky.

Most of the ills in India's governance, if not all, arise from corruption in the government. There was always petty corruption. But it has now spread to the higher echelons of the civil service and the political leadership. With this, the government's ability to control corruption has been seriously compromised. It is not possible to curb corruption in India as long as the electoral and the political system of the country depend on illicit funds. It would seem that elected representatives have no option but to indulge in and support corruption. The cases of Members of the Railway Board and the Chairman of Coal India, the two largest employers in the public sector, are illustrative. How can they be expected to stop corruption in their organisations if they have to pay hefty bribes before their own appointment orders can be issued?

India is one of the fastest growing economies. Some

projections suggest it would be the number one economy in the world by the year 2050. The energy requirements of this bustling economy are increasing rapidly. Coal generates two-thirds of India's power. India is among the top nations of the world in terms of coal reserves and coal production. Coal will continue to be major source of energy for the country. Coal policy and its execution, therefore, is crucial to India's progress. The manner of allocation of coal blocks to private companies in India has been one of the biggest controversies in recent times. The media has referred to it as Coalgate. Open bidding for allocation of this resource was proposed way back in 2004. It does not require great intelligence to understand why it took over eight years to implement a transparent bidding system. The reason is simple and obvious: the entire political class of India was opposed to it.

The Constitution of India, the country's holy book, says that all citizens are equal and that rule of law shall prevail. But the government often acts arbitrarily. Many times, it offers a sense that the political leadership is above the rest of the citizens. Reason, principles, integrity and service are often absent when decisions are taken. Rule of law, a sacrosanct principle of governance, suffers because of widespread corruption which has now spread to even the judiciary. India's judicial system has been reduced to a crawl, at snail's pace. We have ceased to be governed by the rule of law.

India has not been blind to this devastation. Attempts have been made periodically to right this wrong. For instance, the Central Bureau of Investigation (CBI) was set up. The Prevention of Corruption Act was legislated. The Right to Information Act was enforced. And a Lokpal is to be appointed with wide powers. All of these steps are important but they only touch the fringe of the problem. Rule of law is the central instrument. Without that, the mere creation of new institutions and laws cannot provide India with good governance. All institutions ultimately look to delivery to the civil service that has today lost its credibility. India needs comprehensive political, electoral, administrative and judicial reforms, and an enforceable code of conduct for all agencies of the State.

Greed and corruption has generated such anger in India that even the country's electoral politics appears to have been impacted remarkably. A new political outfit, the Aam Aadmi Party, came into being in 2012 with a core cause: end corruption in the country. The Aam Aadmi Party performed spectacularly well in the 2013 election to the Delhi Assembly. It even formed a minority government against all odds. By doing so, the Aam Aadmi Party wrote a new chapter in India's electoral politics. It has shown, although on a small scale, that elections can be contested and won without spending a fortune. It is unfortunate that the Aam Aadmi government lasted only 49 days. There were several question marks on its ability to govern because its ministers had no previous experience and because of its own populist agenda. However, Arvind Kejriwal, the head of the Aam Aadmi Party, and his team would have done a better service to the nation if their electoral success can trigger introspection and churning in mainstream political parties and force them into political and electoral reform. If the need for illicit money, for electoral success, can be curtailed, India could have a new breed of political leaders who value a civil service based on honesty and independence. It might usher in a new era of healthy and harmonious relations between the elected representatives and the civil servants in the overall interest of good governance.

Hyderabad
April, 2014

PC Parakh

Acknowledgements

Grateful thanks to my service colleagues Mr Mohammed Shafiq-Uz-Zaman and Mr BP Acharya and to my brother-in-law Mr AK Bhandari for going through the script and for their valuable suggestions. I also thank Mr Acharya for his cartoon illustrations.

I thank Mr Vijay Simha for his editing and his professional competence. I also thank Mr Vivek Garg and his team at Manas Publications. They have worked very hard and completed the work within weeks of my handing over the script.

My sincere thanks to Mr TSR Subramanian. With his vast experience in the turbulent state of Uttar Pradesh and the Central Government at the highest level of civil service, he has exhibited his deep insight into the governance issues while writing the foreword.

One person, who has been a close witness to all the events recorded in this book, is my wife Usha. Throughout our married life she has been a constant guide and support. Her intuitive wisdom has been invaluable in my work and life. Credit goes to my daughter Sushmita for her inputs across various aspects of making of this book.

And finally, I express my gratitude to an overriding

providence that enabled me to live a life in accordance with the values that I had set for myself.

Hyderabad
April, 2014

PC Parakh

Part One

WITH THE STATE GOVERNMENT

1. Welcome to Andhra Pradesh

After completing my Masters in Applied Geology from the University of Roorkee (now IIT Roorkee), I joined the National Mineral Development Corporation (NMDC) as a Mining Geologist. I had never thought of the civil service as a career option. While working at Khetri Copper Mines, one of my colleagues, Mr HS Madan, was preparing for the civil service examination. At his cajoling, I also entered the fray. As luck would have it, I qualified for the Indian Administrative Service (IAS). As I look back, a career in the civil service, although poorly paid, has been far more satisfying than any other occupation I could have chosen. Perhaps no other profession offers such a wide canvas to work on, as does the Indian Administrative Service. The overall perspective and broad understanding of the issues of governance that this service provides is unparalleled. There are a variety of assignments with State and Central governments—and opportunities to interact and work with a large number of persons in various fields of human activity. One could engage with a poor worker, a billionaire industrialist, a village Sarpanch or even the Prime Minister. It now appears that destiny had scripted my career. I entered the service from the mining industry. My last posting too was in the mining sector where my academic background helped me understand the coal industry better.

In June 1969, after receiving my appointment orders, I joined as an IAS probationer at the Lal Bahadur Shastri National Academy of Administration, Mussoorie. Allotment orders to state cadres were received after a couple of weeks; seven of us were allotted to Andhra Pradesh. Only one of the seven came from Andhra Pradesh. The remaining six were from Rajasthan, Uttar Pradesh, Bihar and Orissa (now Odisha).

We reported to the Chief Secretary at Hyderabad after completing the first phase of training at the Academy. Those of us who were not from Andhra Pradesh were apprehensive about how we would live and work in a state whose culture and language was alien to us. We were placed under the charge of Mr A Valliappan, who was then Deputy Secretary (Political) in the General Administration Department. Mr Valliappan was a warm and friendly person with a charming and loud laugh. He made us feel absolutely at home and made our month's stay at Hyderabad extremely comfortable. We frequently met with him; some of the concerns we had about working and living in an unfamiliar environment melted away in the face of his warmth and affection.

The IAS Officers Association invited us to tea one evening for an informal interaction with senior colleagues. We felt as if we were part of a well-knit and friendly community. Our interaction with senior colleagues at this get-together created a very positive impression about Andhra Pradesh, now our adopted state.

We were required to call on the Governor, the Chief

Minister and the Chief Secretary as part of the protocol. Mr K Brahmananda Reddy was the Chief Minister. We had an appointment with him at 10 AM at his official residence Anand Nilayam. Precisely at the appointed time, we were ushered into his office. Mr Reddy received us with the warmth of a statesman. He spent over half an hour with us, making detailed enquiries about the background of each one of us and telling us what he expected from us as members of the Indian Administrative Service. Before we took leave of him he made a statement, which is still fresh in my mind. He said, "From now on you do not belong to Rajasthan, Uttar Pradesh, Bihar or Orissa. All of you now belong to Andhra Pradesh. The development of our state and the welfare of its people will depend upon your abilities and hard work. I am sure you will prove worthy of my confidence. If you have any problems or difficulty at any time, my doors are always open for you."

These words from the Chief Minister cleared away any

hesitation we had about our future in our adopted state. Like most leaders of that era, Mr Reddy had a broad national outlook, which was far from the parochial thinking common in political leadership of many states today. Working in Andhra Pradesh was a rewarding and satisfying experience. I received respect and affection from the political leadership, colleagues, staff and the people at large, in whatever capacity and in whichever region of the state I worked.

2. Sub-Collector, Asifabad: The First Lesson

I was posted as Sub Collector, Asifabad, in Adilabad district after the completion of my district training. Asifabad, the headquarters of the Subdivision, was a village with a population of about 7,000. There was no minister or MP from Asifabad except for a brief period when Mr Bhim Rao, a tribal MLA was Minister of Tribal Welfare. Members of the Legislative Assembly and Panchayat Samithi Presidents were courteous. They carried themselves with dignity and did not make unjust or unreasonable demands. They did not interfere in the administration.

When I reported at Asifabad, the Collector at Adilabad was a Muslim officer from an aristocratic family. During his entire tenure he never visited my office or any of my Tahsil offices to review my work. His visits to my jurisdiction were merely for shikar (hunting) in the forests of Sirpur area. In the absence of supervision or guidance from the Collector, I was on my own in running the affairs of the division.

On his transfer, an officer promoted from the Subordinate Revenue Service was posted as Collector. Soon after he took charge he chaired a meeting of the district's revenue officers. In the review meeting, he exhorted officers to work honestly and diligently. After the meeting, when I formally called on him, he informed me about his proposed tour of my subdivision. He asked me to advise my Tahsildar not to make elaborate arrangements during his tours.

There wasn't a single hotel or restaurant in all my three Tahsil headquarters from where hygienically-cooked food could be arranged during the visits of ministers or officers. During the visits of VIPs, the local Revenue Inspector would purchase provisions and a trained peon would cook. A touring officer would normally be accompanied by a Camp Clerk (Private Secretary), a Daffedar (Head Peon) and a driver. Some officers paid for their accommodation and food an amount equal to their daily allowance. Others did not. The local revenue officers had to meet the boarding and lodging expenses of touring VIPs and their staff.

I conveyed the instructions of the Collector to my Tahsildars. When the Collector was on his first visit to Asifabad, I went to call on him in the guest house. Dinner was being served. To my utter surprise, half a dozen meat and fish dishes were laid on the dinner table for one individual. After the Collector left, I asked the Tahsildar why such a lavish dinner was cooked for the Collector when he wanted a simple meal. The Tahsildar, who had seen many Collectors in over 30 years, smiled at my naiveté and told me that the Collector's food preferences were ascertained and food served accordingly. This Collector soon acquired notoriety for his corruption. He would collect money at every possible opportunity, including transfers and postings.

One day, I received a letter from the Collector, along

with a representation from the Village Officers, complaining that money was being unofficially deducted from their salary. On inquiry from the Tahsildar the allegations were found to be true. The Tahsildar informed me that every month, money was deducted from the salary of the village officers to meet expenses of touring officers and ministers and other incidental costs. He had kept an account of the income and expenditure from this fund. To my horror, I found that most of the money was being spent on the Collector's household and some on the visits of the minister. Kagaznagar was the only big town in the district with a good bakery. The Collector's household would regularly order supply of bakery products and other items to the Tahsildar Asifabad. I sent my inquiry report to the Collector, informing him that the allegations made in the petition were true. I added that as long as the Tahsildar was responsible for providing hospitality to touring dignitaries, and no funds are officially available, it was not possible to stop illegal collection of funds. The Collector did not reply.

My next Collector was Mr RKR Gonela, a young officer who had just reverted to the state cadre after a stint with the Government of India as Under Secretary. In sharp contrast to the previous Collector, Mr Gonela was scrupulously honest and rule-bound. He banned the use of official vehicles for private purposes. The Officers Club at Adilabad was deserted as there was hardly an officer with his private car. Mr Gonela never availed the hospitality of local Tahsildars. He always insisted on food being brought from a local hotel, and he would pay for his food.

During Mr Gonela's tenure, a Member of the Board of Revenue arrived for a review meeting. A meeting of all the revenue officers of the district was organised at Nirmal (headquarters of another subdivision in the district). The Collector had directed that during the visit of the Member, a simple contributory vegetarian lunch would be arranged and all officers would contribute towards the cost of lunch. It should not be a burden on the Tahsildar, the Collector said.

The Member arrived a little before lunch and went to his room. I believe he was fond of whisky and used to have a peg or two before every meal. After having his drink he joined us for lunch. The lunch was anything but simple. A huge spread of vegetarian and non-vegetarian dishes was laid. Everyone had a sumptuous lunch and the Member retired for his afternoon siesta. Late in the afternoon he started the review meeting that lasted for less than an hour.

Mr Bansilal, PA to the Collector (a senior Deputy Collector and Additional District Magistrate in the Collectorate was designated as PA to Collector those days) was in-charge of the arrangements. After the Member left, I asked Mr Bansilal why such a lavish lunch was served against the directions of the Collector. Mr Bansilal said, "Collector sahib is still new to the job and does not have practical experience of dealing with senior officers. Mr Sinha loves his scotch and good food. Without scotch and a sumptuous lunch, the review meeting would have lasted till midnight with a damning report on our performance."

The Tahsildars or the District Officers of the department concerned were expected to make arrangements for the comfortable stay of visiting senior officers and ministers. Few officers and none of the ministers paid for the hospitality extended to them. During the visits of the Chief Minister and other senior ministers, a large number of party workers and their followers used to join as uninvited guests. There was no official budget for meeting these expenses. It was customary to make the most resourceful, and thus the most corrupt, officer as the Tahsildar at the headquarters so that the desired quality of hospitality could be extended to visiting VIPs.

This system has been in existence from pre-independence days. Everyone knows about it and it has not changed over the years. No one has ever questioned this system and all of us who worked as District Collectors have acquiesced. Every officer who joins the subordinate service is initiated into these malpractices from the beginning of his career and they slowly graduate into bigger corruption.

I was aware of small corruption taking place in Tahsil offices but did not know of a similar practice in my office almost until half way through my stay at Asifabad. The Collector's powers to grant license for a certain category of weapons under the Arms Act were delegated to the Sub-Collector in Adilabad district, because of its large geographical area and poor road connectivity. One day, a person whose gun license I had approved about a month ago approached me with the complaint that his license had not been issued. When I inquired, I found that the file lay with the office typist for more than a fortnight. He had no reason to keep this paper pending for that long. On further inquiry, I discovered that there was a practice of collecting ₹ 100 as bribe for every gun license issued from my office. It was distributed between the head clerk, the dealing clerk, the typist and the peon. As the typist wanted a higher share of the bribe, which the others were not willing to concede, the typist decided to withhold the order. Though no charge of bribery could be proved, disciplinary action was taken against the typist for negligence in performance of his duties.

This kind of institutional corruption exists in almost all departments of the government. Those unwilling to join in are either sucked into it over a period of time or are bypassed. At times, they are even penalised. But the system continues to thrive.

3. Commercial Taxes: The Milch Cow

After completing my initial district postings as Sub-Collector and Joint Collector, I was posted as Deputy Commissioner of Commercial Taxes in early 1975. My charge included the districts of Chittoor and Kadapa. Chittoor shared borders with Tamil Nadu and Karnataka. The Commercial Taxes Department maintained check-posts at the interstate borders to ensure that goods that move into or out of the state were taxed. Since the check-posts had the reputation of being dens of corruption, I used to make frequent surprise inspections. During one of these visits to the check post on the Tamil Nadu border, I noticed in the records that a large number of trucks transported liquor from Pondicherry (now Puducherry) to Yanam via this check-post. Since Chittoor was not on the direct route to Yanam from Pondicherry, I was a tad intrigued. Besides, Yanam was a small village and even if every citizen of Yanam was a drunkard, it would be impossible for such large quantity of liquor to be consumed in Yanam.

I instructed the Assistant Commercial Tax Officer (ACTO) at the check post to follow the next liquor truck that came from Pondicherry. One midnight the ACTO called to inform me that a truck meant for Yanam was being unloaded in Chittoor. I drove to the town police station, picked up the Station House Officer (SHO) and two police constables, and went to the site of unloading. By the time we reached, the truck had been unloaded and cases of liquor were being moved from the footpath to a nearby warehouse. I got the SHO to seal the warehouse. The next day I began investigation. I got a list of all liquor consignments that passed through the Chittoor check-post for a year and sent an officer to verify the records of the interstate check-post at the Yanam border in East Godavari district. It was found that none of those trucks had passed through the Yanam check post. It was thus clear that a large quantity of liquor purporting to be transported from Pondicherry to Yanam was actually being sold in different districts of Andhra Pradesh to evade excise duty and sales tax.

Since it was not possible to find details of the traders to whom delivery of liquor was made, it was decided to treat Pondicherry dealers as casual traders in Andhra Pradesh. I went to Pondicherry to investigate. I requested the Chief Secretary of Pondicherry to help recover the tax due to Andhra Pradesh. Mr Parthasarthy, an officer of Assam cadre who was then Chief Secretary, was candid. He said the liquor trade formed a large part of revenue for Pondicherry and the state could not forego this by curbing the trade. The large difference in tax rates between Andhra Pradesh and Pondicherry was a huge incentive for this illicit activity.

Traders who do not have a registered place of business but bring commodities for sale in Andhra Pradesh could be assessed to sales tax as casual traders. We therefore issued notices to the Pondicherry dealers for assessment of tax based on the records of the check-posts. The traders filed a writ petition in the High Court of Madras against the show cause notice. A single-judge bench of the Madras High Court stayed operation of the notice without issuing notice to the Assessing Officer. After considerable effort I was able to get the stay order vacated. The traders then filed an appeal before a two-judge bench which again issued a stay order. Eight years later, when I was posted to the Commercial Taxes Department in a higher capacity, this stay order was still in operation. Eight years is a long time for traders to wind up and restart business in new names. Successor officers may not show similar interest in contesting the cases. The government may thus lose cases by default. Long delays in the disposal of court cases often lead to loss of revenue for the State.

Although I was unable to collect tax for the prior period because of the court order, our current revenue from the liquor trade increased substantially with the curb on illicit flow of liquor from Pondicherry. A senior Congress leader from the district was the kingpin of this smuggling racket. It appears that he approached the then Chief Minister Mr Vengal Rao for my transfer. Mr Prakash Rao, a long time Private Secretary to Mr Vengal Rao, narrated this incident to me. I believe Mr Vengal Rao chided the Congress leader for making such an unreasonable request. This shows how chief ministers back then were able to resist political pressure and protect and support honest and conscientious officers.

I had a second stint in the Commercial Taxes Department when I was posted as Joint Commissioner in a newly created enforcement wing in the department. Mr K

Chakravarthy, who later resigned from the IAS to take over as Registrar of the Sathya Sai Institute of Higher Learning, was the Commissioner of Commercial Taxes. He wanted the enforcement wing to be independent of territorial officers. It was mandated to make commodity-wise studies, collect intelligence and conduct inspections and raids on business premises. He permitted me to pick officers of my choice.

It is difficult to find officers with total integrity in the Commercial Taxes Department, as corruption in the department is systemic and institutionalised. It is customary for businesses to pay bribes at the time of annual assessment. Officers who are satisfied with this normative annual payment, and who do not indulge in extortion by using their powers, are considered honest. After personal inquiries and scrutiny of confidential records of several officers, my batch-mate Mr MC Mahapatra, who was posted as Secretary to the Commissioner, and I short-listed officers for the enforcement wing. All the officers, once appointed to the enforcement wing, worked with missionary zeal and in a short span of time the enforcement wing acquired a reputation for honesty and professionalism. Inspections and raids were meticulously planned after detailed study of trade practices, scrutiny of check-post data and collection of intelligence.

One incident is worth recounting because it explains how the overall political, administrative and social environment influences individual behaviour and promotes tax evasion and black money. Begum Bazar in Hyderabad is a major wholesale market for food grain, pulses and spices. Our studies revealed substantial evasion of tax on these commodities. We identified a few big traders in this line of business and conducted simultaneous inspection and searches. These inspections confirmed our suspicion of the large-scale evasion of tax on these commodities.

A few days later, a person by the name of Mr Kimtee came to meet me on behalf of his son who was in the pulses business. He was candid and accepted that our assessment and demand of tax was not unreasonable. However, he had come to give me a lesson in how business in food grain and pulses is carried out. He came to tell me why it was not possible to do honest business and pay taxes. Mr Kimtee explained that they were in the wholesale business and operated on a margin of ₹ 2 a bag. Sales tax on each bag was ₹ 20. He said that unless everyone in the business complied with law and paid tax, it is not possible for an individual trader to pay full tax and remain in the business.

He added that tax not paid to the government does not automatically translate into profit for a trader. Most consumers prefer to pay a lower price rather than insist on bills and pay tax. A part of the tax evaded goes in payment of bribes to officials of Sales Tax, Income Tax, Civil Supplies, Municipal Corporation, Police etc., who can complicate things if their demands were not met. Apart from this, musclemen and politicians have to be kept happy. The government has no mechanism by which it can protect trade and business from this. A trader cannot constantly fight these elements and yet survive in the business. An easy and perhaps the only option a trader has is to compromise with the system and use it to his advantage.

Mr Kimtee then took out a bunch of press clippings from his bag on the infamous cement scandal involving the then Chief Minister of Maharashtra, Mr AR Antulay. He asked me how small traders could operate honestly and pay taxes in a corrupt environment where a chief minister was involved in massive corruption and still had the full support of the Prime Minister. Tax evasion, Mr Kimtee said, was a complex socio-economic and political problem that inspections and raids would not solve.

While agreeing with the logic of his argument, I told Mr Kimtee I had no illusions that I could completely or even partially stop tax evasion. My duty as an enforcement officer was to put in my best efforts as long as I held that office. Despite the soundness of his argument, he would have to pay the tax assessed. The best I could do in the circumstance was to reduce the penalty from five times of tax to one time, which was in my discretion.

Tax evasion is not the result of an insatiable urge to maximise income, although greed is a contributing factor. A complex set of factors over which an individual has no control lead people into tax evasion. If the political system depends upon black money, there will be pressure on trade and industry to generate black money. If corruption is widespread in the bureaucracy, black money will be required for statuary clearances and other services. If there is widespread evasion of commodity tax, a business may not survive in an uneven competition. Services such as real estate may be available only in the black-market. Apart from this, the social stigma attached to tax evasion and the severity and certainty of legal sanctions could play an important role in tax compliance. India scores poorly on all these parameters and hence tax evasion and black money is rampant.

4. Civil Supplies: Oily Matters

The early 1980s were days of serious shortage of most of the essential commodities in the country. The Government of India was allotting imported palm oil, palmolein, and rapeseed oil for distribution under the Public Distribution System (PDS).

After I took over as Director, Civil Supplies, I found that the Government of India was allotting equal quantities of palmolein and rapeseed oil to the state. Consumers in Andhra Pradesh did not like rapeseed oil, which has a pungent smell. It was the preferred oil in eastern India and parts of North India. I therefore, wrote to the Government of India not to allot rapeseed oil to Andhra Pradesh and increase our quota of palmolein instead.

In spite of our request, the government allotted 5,000 tonnes rapeseed oil to the state. Although there was no demand, a number of millers landed at my office seeking allotment of this oil for PDS. I submitted a detailed note to Mr P Sitapathi, Commissioner, Civil Supplies, suggesting that we may allot this oil to the millers either in the ratio of their past performance or with reference to their refining capacity. The commissioner returned the file with a one-page noting that neither agreed nor disagreed with my proposal. Since his noting did not make sense to me, I went to discuss it with him. He did not discuss the matter but simply asked me to keep the file pending. While the Commissioner was on tour, I received a call from the Secretary to the Chief Minister, Mr S Santhanam, enquiring why allotment of oil was being delayed. I informed him that the Commissioner has not passed orders. He asked me to bring the file to him. He recorded a noting on the file saying the Chief Minister desires that the oil may be allotted to the three millers listed by him in the file. While returning the file he told me that as Secretary to the Chief Minister he was not Secretary to the government. He was therefore only recording what the chief minister desired. If the Commissioner, who was also the *ex-officio* Secretary to the Government, thought that the orders were wrong, he was free to discuss the matter with the chief minister or re-circulate the file with his recommendations.

On his return from tour, I gave the file to the Commissioner with the noting of the Secretary to the Chief Minister and also communicated his oral advice. Now, the Commissioner shared his dilemma with me. He said the chief minister wanted oil to be allotted to only three select millers when there were many applicants. Mr Sitapathi was an honest officer and did not want to take a wrong decision. But he also didn't want to annoy the Chief Minister. He was quite relieved with a written communication from the CM's office. Orders were accordingly issued allotting the entire quantity to the three millers.

The next day the High Court stayed the allotment. The millers who did not get the allotment approached the High

Court and brought a stay order. Nothing happened for a month. Then, all the millers approached me with a letter saying they had arrived at an understanding for the *pro rata* distribution of oil to all the millers and had decided to withdraw the writ pending in the High Court.

While the matter was pending in the High Court, I asked around to understand why there was such a scramble for allotment of oil that consumers didn't like. I learned that the rapeseed oil which was being allotted under PDS for ₹ 6,000 a tonne had a ready market in Calcutta (now Kolkata) at ₹ 13,000 a tonne. Since there was no demand for this oil in Andhra Pradesh, it was being transported from the Visakhapatnam port to West Bengal for sale in the black market at a huge premium.

Based on the compromise petition and withdrawal of the writ petition, the oil was *pro rata* allotted to all the millers. Having understood the *modus operandi* of the millers, I incorporated a condition while issuing the allotment order. I said the District Supply Officer concerned would inspect the oil—after it was received at the miller's premises and before it was released to fair price shops.

For the first time, rapeseed oil was brought to the millers' premises. As expected, there was no off-take of rapeseed oil from the PDS. After a couple of weeks the millers came up with a representation to sell the oil in the open market claiming that if stored any longer, it would become rancid and unfit for human consumption. I submitted a note to the Commissioner that the millers were aware there was no demand for rapeseed oil in the PDS and yet wanted its allotment. Since oil is meant for PDS, millers could not be allowed to sell it in the open market.

Mr Sitapathi was transferred before he could pass the

orders. The first file the new Commissioner signed was on rapeseed oil. He recorded a note to the effect that since there was no off-take of rapeseed oil through the PDS, further storage would render the oil unfit for human consumption. In a situation of acute shortage, it would be in public interest to allow the millers to sell the oil in the open market. It was true that further storage would have rendered the oil rancid but public interest would have been better served by handing over the oil to the AP Civil Supplies Corporation for sale by open auction, instead of allowing millers to reap undue profit.

Many years later, when I was with the Sales Tax Department, Mr Rajgopal, Secretary of the Andhra Pradesh Oil Millers Association, told me that while millers had paid only a few lakh rupees for getting allotment of oil, they had to spend a few lakh more to be able to sell the oil in the open market. This was because of the condition included in the allotment order.

But things were getting clearer now. With the change in the Chief Minister, the process of transferring inconvenient officers had begun.

5. Collector and District Magistrate: The Ego of Factions

In May 1980, I was posted as the District Collector, Kurnool. In those days Andhra Pradesh had no worthwhile opposition party and all the MLAs in Kurnool were from the Indian National Congress. However, the district was ridden with factionalism and different groups did not see eye to eye. It was, therefore, important for the Collector to keep himself equidistant from all factions.

A few months after I joined at Kurnool, there was a change in government. Dr M Channa Reddy resigned and Mr T Anjaiah took over as the Chief Minister. Mr Anjaiah had a jumbo cabinet and Kurnool got three cabinet ministers, representing different factions within the Congress. Mr Rambhoopal Reddy was Minister of Revenue, Mr E Ayyapu Reddy was Minister of Law and Mr KE Krishnamurthy was Minister of Minor Irrigation. The district was affected by drought and the Minister of Revenue toured the drought-affected parts for three days. Protocol required that the Collector accompany the Chief Minister and the Revenue Minister during tours in the district. Accordingly, I accompanied the Revenue Minister. Within a few days the Law Minister also proposed a tour of the drought-affected areas and wanted me to accompany him. I called on the minister at the Circuit House and informed him that since I had already accompanied the Revenue Minister for three days, the Joint Collector would accompany him during his tour. The minister was not pleased but he reluctantly agreed to the suggestion.

Since elections to the Panchayati Raj Institutions had not been held for some time, in the absence of the elected head of the Zilla Parishad, the government decided to nominate one of the ministers as in-charge for each district to review development works. Mr Ayyapu Reddy, as the senior most, was nominated minister in-charge of Kurnool.

For his first visit after being nominated as the minister in-charge, I deputed the Revenue Divisional Officer (Deputy Collector), Kurnool, to wait at the Circuit House to receive the minister. He was to inform me as soon as the minister arrived so that I could call on him. The minister was however unhappy that when he arrived, the Collector and the Superintendent of Police (SP) were not present to receive him. I explained to the minister that according to protocol, the Collector and the SP were required to receive only the Governor, the Chief Minister and the Revenue Minister on arrival. Other ministers could summon the Collector and the SP if they had specific issues to be discussed. Normally, the district officer concerned with the portfolio of the minister would receive and attend to the minister. However, since Mr Reddy was the Minister of Law and there was no district officer to wait on him, I suggested that in future the headquarters Tahsildar would wait at the Circuit House to receive him. However, the minister did not like this suggestion and our relations were strained from the beginning.

Because of the factions in the district, it was common practice for political leaders to seek transfers and postings of their favourites. Mr Ayyapu Reddy also had some requests that could not be complied with. The National Rural Employment Programme (NREP) or Food for Work Programme, as it was known then, was an important programme for creating rural infrastructure. The sale of rice provided under this programme by the contractors in the open market, in connivance with government officers, was not uncommon. One of the Block Development Officers (BDO) of the district from the minister's community was caught in the act of selling rice. I thought it was a fit case for placing the BDO under suspension pending inquiry. However, the minister wanted the officer to be let-off with a warning. I proposed that the government place the officer under suspension. But the minister used his influence to ensure the officer was not suspended. He was transferred to faraway district of Srikakulam.

The two quarterly meetings the minister presided over passed without trouble. However, under the facade of cordiality at these meetings, I could sense an acute dislike the minister harboured against me. We had no communication outside these review meetings.

When I visited Hyderabad, I thought it appropriate to meet the Chief Secretary and brief him about the uneasy relations between the minister in-charge of the district and I. During my meeting with the Chief Secretary, Mr SR Ramamurthy, I suggested he transfer me from Kurnool because of my uneasy relationship with the minister. The Chief Secretary did not think it good enough reason for a transfer.

Construction at the Nandyal Co-operative Sugar Mills,

the largest industrial investment in Kurnool in recent years, was completed. Because of its importance, the management committee, with the Collector as chair, decided to invite the Chief Minister for the inauguration of the mill.

After meeting the Chief Secretary, I called on the Chief Minister, Mr T Anjaiah, to request him to inaugurate the sugar mill. He readily agreed and gave a date the following month. After confirming this from the Chief Minister, I went to Mr Ayyapu Reddy to request him to preside over the function. He received me in his camp office. I informed him that the Chief Minister had agreed to visit Kurnool and inaugurate the sugar mill and requested his consent to preside over the function. I was totally taken aback by his reaction. He asked how I could directly invite the Chief Minister without his permission. I told him that, as I understood, there was nothing wrong in my inviting the Chief Minister without consulting the minister. I suggested that since the Chief Minister had agreed to inaugurate the mill, it would be appropriate that as minister-in-charge of the district, he presides over the function. The minister said he had no reason to attend the event if I was administering the district like a king without consulting him. He also alleged that I had been indulging in corruption and a Block Development Officer had supplied cement for the construction of my house at Hyderabad. I was shocked by this totally baseless and false allegation from the minister. I advised him to make a formal complaint to the Chief Secretary or the Vigilance Commissioner and left.

After such a hostile reaction from the minister, I thought it was time to reiterate my request for transfer lest our strained relations should spill out in public and embarrass the government. I wrote to the Chief Secretary immediately after I returned to Kurnool.[1]

Mr Reddy accompanied the Chief Minister in his helicopter and attended the inaugural function of the sugar mill. Before returning to Hyderabad the Chief Minister called me to his room. He said while he had received good reports about my work from all the political leaders of the district, Mr Ayyapu Reddy the minister in-charge of the district, was not happy with me. I explained the reasons for Mr Reddy's resentment and suggested that, in view of the estranged relations between us, it would be appropriate that I move out of the district. The Chief Minister appreciated my suggestion and offered to post me in another district of my choice. I, however, requested that he post me back in Hyderabad. In a couple of weeks I received orders posting me as Joint Commissioner of Commercial Taxes.

Although Mr Anjaiah was not highly educated, and rose from an ordinary industrial worker to the position of the Chief Minister, I was deeply impressed by the way he handled my transfer from Kurnool. Unlike his predecessor Dr Channa Reddy, who was known to make telegraphic transfers, it was graceful of Mr Anjaiah to take me into confidence, listen to my point of view, give me an option and then transfer me. He could have transferred me without speaking to me, but it would have left me with a sense of victimisation, as if the transfer was punishment for not following the dictates of Mr Ayyapu Reddy.

---

1. Annexure 5-I.

6. Municipal Corporation of Hyderabad: The First Rebellion

In early October 1982 I was posted as the Special Officer and Commissioner, Municipal Corporation of Hyderabad (MCH). It was one of the most eventful and also the most frustrating assignments of my career.

While working in the Commercial Taxes Department, I had seen how businessmen operate to deprive the government of legitimate revenue by evading payment of taxes. I also noticed that the political, social and economic reality of our country is such that it is almost impossible to conduct business honestly. However, it was my first exposure to how public servants misuse authority to squander public funds, for self-aggrandisement or to enrich themselves.

For quite some time, elections to the MCH had not been held. The Commissioner was also designated as the Special Officer and was empowered to discharge all functions of the elected body. He, therefore, had full powers to sanction all capital and revenue expenditure. When I joined the Corporation, I found that a number of capital works were under execution without reference to the capital budget or available resources. Numerous bills of the contractors were pending for payment and the corporation had no funds to clear these bills.

Large amounts of money had been spent on widening of roads but these roads could not survive even one monsoon. By end of the monsoon almost the entire widened portion was eroded, exposing the underlying road metal. I, therefore, requested the Chief Engineer, National Highways Department, to investigate the road-widening works. The investigation revealed startling facts. The metal used in the construction was uniformly oversized, consolidation was grossly inadequate, crest thickness was only 50 per cent of estimates and the bitumen used was as low as 28 per cent of the quantity check-measured.

Within weeks of my joining the MCH, I received a file seeking approval of estimates for urgent repairs to a road in the Old City and award of the contract on nomination. The Moharram procession was to pass through this road and hence the urgency. I observed that if the repair was linked to the Moharram festival, it could not have been an emergency and should have been proposed well in advance. However, in view of the urgency, I directed that the work may be awarded through a short notice tender. Within hours the file came back indicating difficulties in the issue of short notice tender and seeking approval for nomination. I was intrigued by the insistence on nomination although there was enough time for issue of a short notice tender. I therefore, decided to inspect the road. To my surprise, I found that the entire route through which the Moharram procession was to pass was a good concrete road that needed no repairs. It was obviously a fake estimate to make money. It was later revealed by the Chief Engineer that such estimates were routinely prepared every year on the eve of Moharram and money so sanctioned was given to local political leaders.

Another example of the complicity of contractors and engineers emerged during an investigation into the construction of a deck slab over a major drain that crosses Road No. 1, Banjara Hills, one of the up-market residential areas of Hyderabad. The concrete deck slab constructed only a year ago had started to crumble. In order to investigate this, we decided to get core samples of the deck slab for analysis. However, when the team of the officers went to collect samples, it could not collect even a single sample of the entire thickness of the slab. The quality of construction was so poor that the sample would crumble into pieces and fall into the drain. With great difficulty, some pieces of concrete were collected and sent to the laboratory. The results were alarming. The slab thickness was only 60 per cent of what was check-measured and the cement and steel used in the construction was only a fraction of the estimate.

As I dug more into the working of the MCH, I found maladministration and corruption everywhere. Assessment and collection of property tax was totally arbitrary. There were no well-defined parameters to assess tax and the amount of tax payable was entirely at the discretion of tax officers. Variation in tax liability of similar buildings was as high as 500 per cent. Garbage disposal was unscientific and unhealthy for workers, fleet utilisation was woefully low, there was large-scale pilferage of fuel, the overloaded drainage system was choking for want of scientific management, and city planning was reduced to mere grant of relaxation from the Building Rules.

I took a few steps after a detailed study of the working of different divisions of the MCH. The Central Road

Research Institute was involved in training of engineers on execution of road works, a more rational property tax system was evolved that was based on scientific classification of properties with reference to their location, size and type of contraction, Tata Consultancy Services was engaged to computerise the assessment and collection of property tax, the Administrative Staff College of India was requested to take up a works and methods study to improve labour productivity of conservancy staff, and the National Building Organisation was approached to adopt low cost technology for slum housing.

In January 1983, elections took place to the Andhra Pradesh Assembly. Mr NT Rama Rao floated a new party the Telugu Desam Party and fought the election on the twin planks of self-respect for Telugus and eradication of corruption from the government. He swept the polls against all expectations and formed the government.

I had done enough groundwork to control corruption and had sent reports to the government about the state of affairs in the MCH. I had also recommended disciplinary action against some engineers based on my investigations. I was, therefore, quite happy at the change of government. I thought the new Chief Minister would support me in dealing with corruption. I believed so because the promise to eradicate graft was a major contributor to the electoral success of Mr NT Rama Rao.

To my great surprise, instead of hearing of any action against the officers I had reported against, I received orders transferring me from MCH in February 1983 without giving me an alternative posting. To understand the background under which I was transferred, I called on the then Principal Secretary, Municipal Administration, Mr SN Achanta. He was equally surprised at the turn of events and advised me not to handover charge until he discussed the matter with the Chief Secretary and the Chief Minister, who were both away in Delhi.

When I returned to my office after meeting Mr Achanta, there was another order lying on my table, directing me to immediately handover charge to Mr RP Singh, an officer of the 1976 batch, without waiting for my posting. In view of this new development, I spoke to Mr Achanta for his permission to handover charge immediately. I did not want to create an impression that I wanted to hang on to the post after receiving transfer orders.

The post of Special Officer and Commissioner, MCH, is considered a prestigious and important assignment. Any officer posted to this assignment would like to join at the earliest. Mr RP Singh, however, called on me and offered to wait if I wanted to make a request for cancellation of my transfer. Since I had already made up my mind, I thanked him for his gesture and handed-over charge the same day.

There are not many officers of impeccable personal integrity like Mr RP Singh. The fact that even he was transferred from MCH within seven months is testimony to a creeping degeneration in public administration that does not tolerate officers who are unwilling to compromise with principles and values.

I had spent close to sixteen hours every day in the MCH. I used to start at 5 AM with inspection of conservancy staff in different parts of the city, come home for breakfast at 9 AM and be back in office by 10.30 AM. Most days I reached home by 10 PM. I had barely seen my daughter in the four months I was at the MCH. My wife was not too happy with this schedule but was willing to put up with it, for what I thought was in the public interest

Mr NT Rama Rao was new to politics as were most of the ministers including the Minister of Municipal Administration. Therefore, there was no reason to believe that my transfer could be for political reasons. It was clear that the transfer was engineered by people who feared investigation into financial irregularities and corruption in MCH. The sudden transfer with the direction to hand over charge immediately, without even waiting for an alternative posting, as if I had committed a crime, came as a great shock. I was disappointed, humiliated and engulfed with intense frustration. I lost interest in the service and even contemplated resigning from IAS and returning to my profession as a geologist.

In the scheme of personnel management in the government, the CS is responsible for cadre management, postings and transfers of IAS officers. Mr BN Raman was the CS when I was posted to MCH and he continued as the CS when I was posted out. I, therefore, called on him to understand the reason for my transfer from MCH within four months. He did not give me a satisfactory reply apart from saying it was the government's prerogative to transfer and post officers, and that officers are not expected to question the wisdom of the government in these matters.

Since the CS was not able to give me a convincing answer for my transfer, I sought an appointment with the CM. However, despite several requests, I could not meet the CM. I recalled the words of the former Chief Minister Mr Brahmananda Reddy, when we called on him as young probationers, that his doors were always open if we ever had a problem. Times had changed and so had Chief Ministers and Chief Secretaries.

In stark contrast to how the then Chief Minister and Chief Secretary handled my transfer from Kurnool by taking me into confidence, here the Chief Secretary was not even willing to disclose the reasons for a totally unwarranted transfer. I felt it was the responsibility of the Chief Secretary to resist pressures, if any, and advise the Chief Minister appropriately.

After failing to get proper response from the Chief Secretary or the Chief Minister, I thought it appropriate to formally question the wisdom of the government's personnel policy that does not allow officers a reasonable tenure to enable them to conceptualise, plan and execute programmes in public interest. I, accordingly, wrote to the Chief Secretary[2] and released it to the press in order to initiate a public debate.

Over the next two days, almost all the newspapers published from Hyderabad had the contents of my letter in the headlines.[3] These publications generated public debate but had little impact on the government.

I had earlier considered resigning from the service. However, on second thoughts, I decided to fight it out with the government. I, therefore, wrote to Dr LM Singhvi, a noted jurist and constitutional expert, for advice, if I could sue the State Government for causing me mental anguish and acting against public interest.[4] Dr Singhvi was of the opinion that the Law of Torts was in a weak and archaic state in India and it was difficult to make an accurate prognosis about the success of my proposed action.[5] I did

2. Annexure 6-I.
3. Annexure 6-II.
4. Annexure 6-III.
5. Annexure 6-IV.

not have enough money to fight the government without a reasonable chance of success. I however, did not want to continue working with the State Government and opted for central deputation.

The government did not like the release of my letter to the press and called for an explanation for violation of Rule 6 read with Rule 7(1) of the All India Service (Conduct) Rules, 1968, which prohibit members of service from making any statement of facts or opinion to press, which has the effect of an adverse criticism of any policy or action of the government.[6]

I sent a detailed reply to the government, justifying my action on the grounds that my letter released to the press was not adverse criticism of the government.[7] It was constructive criticism that was necessary in public interest. I said that if such constructive criticism amounts to breach of conduct rules, then perhaps such rules need to be changed.

I did not hear anything from the government after this. I presume the government did not proceed with disciplinary action against me, possibly realizing that it had made a mistake and an escalation may cause it further embarrassment.

Decades have passed since I wrote those letters and the situation, instead of improving, has worsened all over the country. I hope the recent Supreme Court order directing the government to enact a Civil Service Law and ensure minimum fixed tenure for civil servants would usher in the required changes in the government's HR policy.

---

6. Annexure 6-V.
7. Annexure 6-VI.

7. Andhra Pradesh Dairy Development Corporation: A Rolling Stone

After working in the Ministry of Petroleum from 1983 to 1988, I reverted to the state cadre in April 1988. Mr NT Rama Rao was still the Chief Minister. I formally called on him. He was quite courteous and asked me if I had preference for any assignment. I replied that I would be happy with any assignment the government may decide.

In early May I was posted as Managing Director of Andhra Pradesh Dairy Development Corporation (APDDC). AP Dairy was the second largest public sector dairy in India after Amul and was doing reasonably well.

While I was still settling down in the job, Mr PL Sanjeev Reddy, who was Secretary to the Chief Minister, referred to me a person with a proposal to sell technology and equipment to produce fodder indoors under controlled climate. He wanted the APDDC to purchase his technology and equipment for production and distribution of green fodder to milk farmers. He made a presentation suggesting that these plants could be set up at our chilling centres. Green fodder could be produced in these plants at about ₹ 1 a kilo.

I informed him that small farmers in the state are not used to buying green fodder. They feed animals with crop

residue and green fodder picked up from the field bunds or fodder grown in their fields, after the main crop has been harvested. It would, therefore, be difficult for the corporation to sell the fodder produced by his technology at that price. As an alternative, I offered to provide vacant land in a few chilling centres at a nominal lease. He could setup a few plants at his cost and demonstrate commercial viability and market potential, before we purchased his technology and equipment. He, however, insisted that the APDDC should procure and setup these units. I received calls from the CM's office a couple of times to accept his proposal. However, I informed the Secretary to the CM that as project *prima facie* does not appear commercially viable, my counter proposal would be more appropriate instead of the corporation investing in the project.

In the last week of July, I received marching orders from the APDDC, again in less than four months from the date of my posting. I do not know if there was a link between my transfer and the fodder machines.

8. Godavari Fertilizers and Chemicals Ltd.: Corrupted Brilliance

In August 1990 I joined as Managing Director of Godavari Fertilizers and Chemicals Limited. The Government of Andhra Pradesh promoted this company along with IFFCO to set up a fertilizer plant (Di-ammonium phosphate or DAP) at Kakinada. The Government of Andhra Pradesh held 26 per cent equity; IFFCO held 25 per cent and 49 per cent was with the public. Unlike most other state public sector undertakings, where directors were appointed for political patronage, this company had outstanding professionals as directors. Dr N Bhanu Prasad, former Chairman of ONGC, and Mr KK Pillai, former Managing Director of VST Industries, represented the public shareholders. Mr M Gopalakrishna, an outstanding officer, was the first Managing Director and remained at the helm from the inception of the project until the plant was commissioned. The State government and IFFCO had to jointly approve all board-level appointments, including that of the Managing Director. This ensured that the company was managed by a competent board.

Mr Gopalakrishna did an excellent job of setting up a state-of-the-art plant and appointing good officers and workers. He had also established a good name for the brand 'Godavari'. However, soon after the plant was commissioned, the company got into a serious crisis. Imports of phosphoric acid, the basic raw material to produce DAP, suddenly stopped because of a dispute with Morocco. Morocco had virtual monopoly of phosphoric acid supply to India. I joined the company during this crisis.

As the company was able to produce only a small quantity of DAP because of scarce imported raw materials, we diverted our attention to marketing of imported fertilizers. Payment was made on the basis of quantity mentioned in the bill of lading (BL) for fertilizers imported in bulk, although the actual quantity on unloading could be more or less than the BL quantity. If it was less than the BL quantity, a claim would have to be made with the insurance company. If it was more than the BL quantity, it would be bonus and add to the profit of the company.

In most shipments handled by GFCL, the discharged quantity was marginally less or more than the BL quantity. In one shipment, we received almost one per cent in excess of the BL quantity. We were extremely happy that this would give us additional profit. However, this was not to be.

The marketing department of the company was headed by a General Manager who was assisted by a Chief Marketing Manager (CMM). The CMM was brilliant. I, therefore, started to rely heavily on him to expand the market share of the company. However, I could not assess the flip side of his brilliance.

Soon after the news of excess quantity in the shipment became known, he conspired to swindle the company along with the managers for Uttar Pradesh and Madhya Pradesh, two major markets of the company. He got false reports generated from UP and MP, saying imported fertilizer bags weighed less by 2 to 3 kilos and needed to be standardised (by adding shortfall to make bags weigh 50 kg.). A note was submitted to me saying the DAP season was fast coming to an end and unless all stocks were liquidated immediately after standardisation, we would be saddled with huge inventory of unsold stock for the entire year. This would lead to huge costs on storage and interest.

Mr P Balasubrahmanyam, a State Civil Service officer on deputation to the company as General Manager (Distribution), was supervising the unloading and bagging operations at Kakinada port. Our stevedoring agent, who had worked with GFCL for a long time, was a person of good repute. There was little possibility of large-scale mischief at the Kakinada end. However, because of the urgency, I dispatched a few officers from Hyderabad to supervise standardisation operations.

I decided to visit two major centres of Allahabad and Varanasi to oversee the operations. The CMM had reached ahead of me. On arrival at Varanasi, I was first taken to Vishwanath Temple where a pooja was organised in which half the day was lost. After that, a visit to two dealers was arranged which, I now realise, was orchestrated by placing a few short-weight bags in the front row to demonstrate the need for standardisation. At Allahabad, after a visit to the premises of a dealer, I wanted to inspect another dealer's premises without advance notice. However, I was told that the other dealer was across the river and we would have to navigate a narrow bridge with heavy traffic. If we ventured there, we may not be able to return in time for our flight. I was unhappy with the way the programme was organised but I did not suspect mischief.

Soon after I returned to Hyderabad, General Manager (Finance), Mr Subramanyam, informed me that he had received a message from one of his executives. Apparently my visit to UP was manipulated. There was no shortage in the bags and no standardisation was being done. The CMM had plotted all this in collusion with the C&F agents and the field staff. I now knew why my programme at Varanasi and Allahabad was organised such that I spend minimum time with dealers. I was taken for a ride.

I immediately asked the CMM to return to Hyderabad and sent the General Managers of Marketing, Distribution and Finance as a fact-finding team to UP and MP. These officers confirmed that all bags received in the North Indian market had full quantity of fertilizer. They discovered that the CMM had conspired with the Regional Manager at Delhi, the managers at Lucknow and Bhopal, and the company's C&F agents in UP and MP.

I quickly divested the CMM of his responsibilities and

constituted a committee of three general managers to make detailed investigation into the entire operation—beginning from the unloading of the ship to the receipt of fertilizers with dealers in the North Indian markets. The committee conclusively established that there was no error in the weight of bags dispatched from the port. It was the work of the CMM along with the managers and C&F agents in UP and MP.

It was a revealing moment. A corrupt officer at a senior level could in a short while motivate and drag an entire hierarchy of an organisation into the cesspool of corruption. But the reverse was also true. An honest functionary in the chain could defeat such designs.

I was in a serious dilemma. I could not take disciplinary action against all the officers who went along with the CMM. That would have paralysed the company. An option was to initiate disciplinary action against the CMM and the managers at Delhi, Lucknow and Bhopal, hold a formal inquiry and terminate their services by applying the Conduct Rules. This would have taken at least six months. We would have to keep crucial marketing posts vacant until a final decision was taken. The company could not afford this.

Another option was to give the offenders three months' salary in lieu of the notice period and terminate their services. This option had drawbacks too. The officers could seek legal redress. The High Court could agree that GFCL was a public sector company and issue a stay order. The matter could then drag on for years. We would have a far bigger problem.

While I was pondering, a news item appeared in newspapers from Hyderabad. It said two MLAs, Mr A Bulli Abbai Reddy and Mr P Subhash Chandra Bose, had submitted a memorandum to the Chief Minister seeking a

CBI probe against Mr Balasubrahmanyam, GM (Distribution), and I. These MLAs called it a ₹1 crore scandal in handling imported fertilizers. The MLAs also demanded our suspension pending investigation.

I was outraged. These two MLAs had never met me or any other officer of the company before making these allegations. Obviously, they had acted at the behest of the CMM without any attempt to ascertain the facts. The CMM thus tried to deflect attention from him and turn the tables on me. This was the first time I learned how MLAs can become willing tools in the hands of corrupt individuals.

I wanted legal action to be taken against the MLAs. I therefore, submitted a note to the Board of Directors proposing the following course of action:

1. Filing of a criminal case against the MLAs under provisions of the Indian Penal Code, for defaming the reputation of the company and its executives.
2. Filing of a libel suit for ₹10 lakh.

The Board agreed. But the Chief Secretary, Mr KV Natarajan, who was *ex-officio* Chairman of the company, did not approve the minutes of the meeting. He directed that the minutes be redrafted in consultation with Mr Williams, one of the government nominees on the board. Mr Natarajan did not agree to my suggestion to place both sets of the minutes for confirmation at the next board meeting. He insisted and approved the minutes as modified by Mr Williams. Instead of seeking immediate legal action against the MLAs, the revised resolution required the Managing Director to take follow-up action at an appropriate time in consultation with the Chairman.

Mr Natarajan had a good reputation as an upright and

courageous officer. I had expected him to support me against the MLAs who had levelled baseless and false allegations. I was surprised by his reluctance to initiate legal action against the MLAs. Perhaps he suspected my integrity. He directed Mr Williams to visit Kakinada and conduct an independent investigation. I was told that Mr Williams tried hard to find evidence against Mr Balasubrahmanyam and I. He could not find any.

The revised board note authorised the Managing Director to take legal action in consultation with the Chairman. I, therefore, submitted a note to Mr Natarajan seeking his consent to initiate legal action. However, Mr Natarajan referred the matter to the government for advice. Perhaps he did not want to bring upon himself the odium of initiating criminal action against MLAs who belonged to the ruling party. The Chair's consent never came. Meanwhile, my tenure at GFCL came to an end on the 31st July 1992. Mr Natarajan retired a little before that.

I decided to act against the marketing executives who indulged in the fraud. I held that GFCL could not be considered a government company because the government held only 26 per cent of the equity. I assessed that the High Court might not entertain a writ against GFCL. Accordingly, I decided to terminate the services of the three executives by paying them three months' salary in lieu of the notice period. When the termination orders were served on the delinquent officers, all of them requested to be permitted to resign instead being terminated from service. I agreed. I wanted to obviate even the remote chance of their seeking legal redress.

After I left GFCL, the company did not take legal action against the MLAs. One of the MLAs, Mr P Subhash Chandra

Bose, later regretted his action. He told the then Collector, Mr Randeep Sudan, who conveyed it to me. Finally, after Mr Natarajan retired, the government agreed to file a criminal complaint on my behalf against the other MLA by appointing a Special Public Prosecutor of my choice. However, even before a complaint could be filed, Mr Daljeet Arora, who had taken over as Chief Secretary, called me to advise that no useful purpose would be served by pursuing a criminal case against the MLA. It could be years before a judgment is pronounced. No one could predict what the court may say. The results might not be commensurate with the energy and time I might be required to spend on the case. While I did not fully agree, I deferred to him and did not insist on a criminal case.

By the time I left GFCL, the company had turned around. It had wiped out its accumulated losses. The workers' expectations for wage revision had spiralled and they went on a month's strike demanding unreasonably high wages and reinstatement of two workers who were dismissed for acts of indiscipline. The management and the unions reached a settlement after a series of meetings on all issues except the reinstatement of the dismissed employees. The unions were adamant on this. Two meetings were held with the then Labour Minister Mr P Janardhan Reddy, who was also a labour leader himself. Mr Reddy insisted on reinstatement of the dismissed workers. I explained the seriousness of the charges against them. I asked him why he insisted on their reinstatement even though he was aware of the serious nature of the charges. He said he was aware of the charges, but it was a matter of his prestige now. If as labour minister he could not ensure the reinstatement of two dismissed workers, what was the use of his being in the post? I pleaded that as labour minister it was also his responsibility to see that industrial units maintained discipline and a healthy work culture. He was unwilling to relent. Ultimately, I had to approach the Chief Minister who persuaded the Labour Minister to drop his totally unacceptable demand.

Despite the strain in relations between the management and the unions during strike period, mutual trust and respect returned soon after the wage settlement was reached. Mr Balasubrahmanyam, who doubled as General Manager (Human Resources), played a crucial role in winning the trust of the workers. Of all the officers I have worked with in my service, Mr. Balasubrahmanyam who rose from a clerical position to IAS stands out as a man with exacting standards of personal integrity. He was a rare combination of honest yet very efficient and effective officer. My faith in his integrity was total and when the MLAs complained against him, I wrote to the government that his integrity is indubitable and I take full responsibility for any acts of commission or omission imputed to him.

The unions appreciated the management's tough stand against corruption and indiscipline. The morale of the workers and the executives was high. There was bonhomie between the union and the management. My farewell at Kakinada and Hyderabad was emotional and touching. There was none of the rancour which existed prior to the strike. The staff and workers union presented me with a roll of honour that I will always cherish.

9. Industries Department: Home Delivery of Bribes

In August 1993 I took over as Commissioner of Industries. A few states had become proactive in investment promotion after the Indian economy was liberalised. No such initiative was, however, taken at the political level in Andhra Pradesh. The department still had the mentality of the license permit raj.

One day, Mr Varaprasad Reddy, founder of Shantha Biotech (now a subsidiary of Sanofi SA, then a start-up), visited me. He had applied for alcohol license for his project. The Commissioner of Industries had to make a recommendation for allocation of alcohol. An Industrial Promotion Officer (IPO) was expected to inspect the industrial unit and submit his report on the need for alcohol. The IPO who visited the unit refused to send his report until his demands were met. On inquiry it was found that having inspected the unit, the IPO did not submit his report and also took the relevant file with him when transferred. I suggested that Mr Reddy make a formal complaint and help us trap the IPO through the Anti-Corruption Bureau. Mr Reddy did not agree. It was understandable because he would not like to waste his time as a witness in prolonged judicial proceedings that would inevitably follow such an action.

When departmental action was initiated against the IPO, he said the relevant file was misplaced in office and, therefore, he could not submit his report and hand-over the file to his successor.

In the absence of a formal complaint from Mr Reddy and his unwillingness to trap the IPO, serious misconduct of corruption had to be treated as mere negligence. The officer could get away with minor punishment. Misplaced sympathy, fear of reprisal and harassment by the department, and waste of time in cumbersome and prolonged judicial proceedings discourage most victims of corruption from filing formal complaints against the corrupt.

In another instance, the Collector of Medak district deliberately delayed the issue of No Objection Certificate (NOC) to an industry for storage of petroleum products. He signed the file only after he received his payoff although I wrote to him and spoke to him on phone. A businessman often prefers to pay a bribe rather than resist. This is because the cost of time wasted in getting regulatory clearances is far more than the cost of bribes. This officer, who was known for corruption, was adept at political management and could indulge in such activities because he knew nothing would happen to him.

When I took over as Commissioner, Mr Vijaya Bhaskara Reddy was the Chief Minister. He was to face elections within a year and did not have much time for industry. The Indian National Congress lost power and in December 1994, Mr NT Rama Rao returned as Chief Minister. He was essentially a welfare-oriented and industry and trade were low on his list of priorities.

After an internal coup in the Telugu Desam Party, Mr Chandrababu Naidu took over as Chief Minister of Andhra Pradesh in September 1995. He was the Minister of Finance and Revenue in Mr Rama Rao's cabinet. He knew it was necessary to promote investment and generate resources to sustain welfare programmes. He brought a new work culture to the government. He could work continuously for long hours without signs of fatigue. He was a keen observer, open to criticism and willing to learn. He had long-term perspective. Under his proactive leadership several steps were taken at the political and bureaucratic level to make the state investor-friendly.

At the bureaucratic level, the biggest hurdle faced by the entrepreneurs was to get clearances from a large number of agencies before a project could be executed. Each department had its own format in which information was to be furnished. Much of it was repetitive and common to all departments. The entrepreneurs were then to follow-up with each department and pay speed money at each point.

It was decided to devise a common application form which would contain information required by every department. This was to be submitted to the Commissioner of Industries who would act as a nodal department and get clearances from all departments. A common format was developed although most departments resisted. It was decided that each department would process the application within four weeks and send clearances to the Commissioner's office. Most departments did not like this as it would eliminate direct contact with entrepreneurs and, thus, scope for collecting bribes.

The departments began to find defects in the application. They returned the form for rectification, close to the time limit of four weeks. The Commissioner's office was then required to correspond with an entrepreneur to seek additional information and clarifications. Instead of solving the problem, it created more problems by introduction of Commissioner of Industries as an additional interface. This further delayed clearances.

A more effective initiation was then taken for faster industrial approvals. A State Investment Promotion Committee (SIPC) was created with the Chief Secretary as Chairman. A State Investment Promotion Board (SIPB) was created with the Chief Minister as Chairman. The SIPC met every month with the secretaries involved in industrial clearances. It was able to effectively cut down delays. Mr K Madhav Rao, who was the Chief Secretary, was proactive and ensured the success of this initiative.

Mr Naidu ensured that the SIPB, with him as Chairman, also met every month to monitor clearances and decide on matters that the SIPC could not decide on. These two initiatives considerably improved the time taken in clearances and considerably reduced the scope for corruption at lower levels. Slowly but surely, the image of the Industries Department changed from that of controller to that of facilitator. The Commissioner of Industries now became the focal point for investment promotion.

In November 1996, I took over as Principal Secretary (Industries). By this time, Mr Naidu had acquired the image of a hardworking and forward-looking CEO. The Confederation of Indian Industry (CII), under the leadership of Mr Tarun Das, became a strong partner for promotion of Andhra Pradesh as an investment destination. Two successful investment promotion tours of the Chief Minister to South East Asia and the USA were organised in collaboration with the CII. They laid the foundation for making Andhra Pradesh in general and Hyderabad in particular a major investment destination. Mr R Chandrasekhar, who was Chairman of the Andhra Pradesh Industrial Infrastructure Corporation, and Mr Randeep Sudan, then Joint Secretary in Mr Naidu's office, were extremely hardworking and intelligent officers. They ably assisted in successfully organising and conducting these tours. A number of big ticket projects such as the High Tech City, the Hyderabad International Airport, private ports on the Andhra Coast, the Outer Ring Road, and the Indian Business School came about because of Mr Naidu's initiatives.

As Principal Secretary, Industries, I was also *ex-officio* Chairman of the Andhra Pradesh Mineral Development Corporation (APMDC). The corporation's major activity was mining and export of barytes. We called for annual tenders for exports. Contractors bid for pithead price to be paid to the APMDC, after which they were responsible for transporting material from the mine stockyard and for delivery of product to the destination. There was severe competition in the tender that year because of high price of barytes in the international market. The price offered was high compared to previous years. The H-1 bidder had the backing of the Congress party while the H-2 bidder was a former Telugu Desam Party MP. There was pressure on the Chief Minister for cancellation of the tender on the grounds that the rate quoted by the H-1 bidder was unworkable. It was argued that he would not be able to execute the contract and the APMDC would lose the export market and suffer heavy losses.

The Chief Minister held a meeting where the H-2 bidder was present. I explained to the Chief Minister that the rates quoted were much higher than previous years but they were still workable. They would leave the contractor with profit although lesser than earlier. In case the contractor failed to perform, we had enough security deposit to safeguard the interests of the APMDC. We could call for fresh short notice tender if H-1 failed to perform. I held that we could not cancel a tender on the presumption that H-1 would fail. I could see an expression of annoyance and displeasure on Mr Naidu's face. However, it should be said to his credit, he did not pressurise me further.

As the rates quoted by the H-1 bidder were high, he was unable to lift the material as per the agreed schedule. I, therefore, asked the remaining bidders to lift the stocks at H-1 rates which they readily agreed to do. The APMDC made a profit of about ₹ 18 crore that year. It was more than the cumulative profit it had made since its incorporation.

I remained Principal Secretary (Industries) until June 1999 when I had to request the Chief Minister for a lighter assignment because of health problems.

During the four years I worked closely with Mr Naidu, a number of important decisions were taken. Except the incident relating to export of barytes, there was no other case where I was pressurised into acting against my judgment. This was in stark contrast to later years when officers in Andhra Pradesh were forced into taking decisions that led them to trouble. Mr Naidu did not believe in frequent transfer of officers; most officers had long tenures. I had a long stint of over six years in the Industries Department, first as Commissioner Industries, and later as Principal Secretary.

The media often reports on large-scale corruption in the government. But there is equal or greater corruption in the private sector that goes unnoticed. While working as

Principal Secretary, Industries, I was a nominee Director of the Government of Andhra Pradesh on the Board of the Andhra Pradesh Paper Mills Limited, a Bangur group company. The government held 26 per cent equity. This company was the largest producer of writing and printing paper in Andhra Pradesh. The company was going in for a major expansion and modernisation programme with large capital investment. The company had called for tenders for purchase of major plant equipment. Prices were under negotiation with vendors.

One evening, the Vice President (Finance), Mr Seetharamaiah, made a social call at my residence. While leaving, he left a plastic bag with a print of Lord Venkateshwara on it. I thought he might have brought some Tirupati prasadam. After Mr Seetharamaiah left, I asked my daughter to keep the prasadam in the fridge. When she looked into the bag she found bundles of currency notes. I immediately called Mr Seetharamaiah and asked him to

return and pick up the bag he had left behind. Mr Seetharamaiah came back, profusely apologised and expressed regret for what he had done. He could not have done this without the explicit approval of the highest in the company.

The next day I sent a letter to the Chairman, Mr LN Bangur, to have independent directors on the board investigate the matter.[8] At the next board meeting, I insisted on removal of Mr Seetharamaiah from the services of the company.

Mr Seetharamaiah later filed a writ petition in the High Court of Andhra Pradesh questioning his removal. A single judge of the High Court, by adopting a convoluted argument, held AP Paper Mills as a public authority and ordered his reinstatement. A person who should have been charged for criminal misconduct, of trying to bribe a civil servant, could misuse the legal system and return to service. Mercifully, on an appeal filed by the company, a two-judge bench set aside the order of the single judge.

Obviously, corruption is not the monopoly of the government. It has infested almost all sectors of our society.

8. Annexure 9-I.

10. Department of Public Enterprises: Political Compulsions

I took charge of the Department of Public Enterprises in July 2000. Most public sector enterprises (PSEs) in Andhra Pradesh, instead of creating surplus for investment and growth, were a drain on the exchequer. Therefore, the World Bank added a condition for financial assistance. They wanted the PSEs to be restructured, a euphemism for closure of sick and chronically loss-making companies and for privatising those that could be rehabilitated. An Implementation Secretariat (IS) was created to assist the State government in this. This secretariat had assistance from the Department for International Development (DFID), UK. As the Principal Secretary (PE), I was *ex-officio* Chairman of the IS.

The Nizam Sugars Limited was one of the major companies slated for privatisation. The Nizam of Hyderabad started it in 1934; it was said to be the biggest sugar mill in Asia at the time. The company had six sugar mills and two distilleries spread over three regions of the state. All these mills were making losses while neighbouring private sugar mills operated profitably.

After evaluating the various options, it was decided to

put each unit of the company for sale through open auction. Two sugar mills and one distillery were successfully privatised. We got a price well above the upset price fixed by the consultants. The people who bought those units were financially sound and experienced in the sugar industry.

The auction of different mills was to be conducted in phases to ensure maximum competition. After the privatisation of three units, while the process of advertising of the main unit at Shakkarnagar was under examination, an unsolicited offer was received from M/s Goldstone Exports Limited (GELCON). The Minister of Sugar wanted the proposal examined.

The government had constituted a Cabinet Committee of Ministers headed by the finance minister to examine and approve privatisation proposals. The ministers from the districts, where the units were located, were special invitees.

I examined the unsolicited proposal of M/s Goldstone Exports. I told the Committee that it was improper to consider an unsolicited offer when the process of tendering is underway. Apart from this, the applicant had no experience of the sugar industry. He was seeking transfer of huge company assets on a promise of meagre investment on his part for revival. The IS consultants concurred with me.

I expected the committee to outright reject the proposal. However, the Chairman decided to invite the applicant to give a presentation. After the presentation made by M/s Goldstone, I reiterated my views for rejection of the proposal. However, the committee advised M/s Goldstone to improve upon its offer.

The Cabinet Committee met half-a-dozen times. At every meeting, Goldstone came up with incremental improvement on its proposal. Each time, I advised rejection of the unsolicited offer. Finally, the committee suggested that the matter be taken up with the Chief Minister for a final decision.

Accordingly, a meeting was held with Mr Chandrababu Naidu. The Finance Minister briefed the Chief Minister on the Goldstone proposal. The Cabinet Committee's views on accepting the offer were also shared. I reiterated my stand. I suggested the unsolicited bid be rejected and open tender be issued. After hearing both sides, the Chief Minister observed that the Goldstone offer should be accepted if all the ministers in the Cabinet Committee and the ministers concerned from the districts are in favour.

I did not expect Mr Naidu to give this verdict. After the ministers left, I told him it would be wrong to accept an unsolicited offer. I said we should follow the established and transparent method of open tender. Mr Naidu agreed but expressed political compulsions for going against my recommendations. He told me that Mr Chandrasekhar Rao had just started a Telangana Party and Panchayat elections were round the corner. At this juncture, he could not afford to go against the wishes of the Telangana ministers who are all in favour of the Goldstone proposal.

Immediately on my return to office, I sent a note to the Chief Secretary informing him that since the Cabinet Committee does not seem to have confidence in me, it would be appropriate for me to leave this assignment so the government could post a suitable officer who enjoys the confidence of the Committee.[9] I applied for earned leave for two months.

---

9. Annexure 10-I.

I am still baffled. How could Goldstone convince an entire group of ministers to accept a proposal which on the face of it was bizarre?

Eventually, the privatisation of Nizam Sugars became a major political issue. A Committee of the Legislative Assembly was appointed to go into the entire process of privatisation. The Cabinet Committee was censured for entertaining the unsolicited offer of M/s Goldstone.[10]

An unconventional approach against the accepted norms of open bid resulted in unnecessary litigation. After a decade, the matter is still pending in the High Court and continues to haunt the State government.

10. Annexure 10-II.

Part Two

MINISTRY OF COAL

11. My First Minister Ms Mamata Banerjee: The Other Side of Simplicity

I was empanelled for posting as Secretary to the Government of India along with my other batch-mates. I knew that intense lobbying is required for senior positions. I never had the instincts of a networker or a lobbyist. I had, therefore, not opted for postings as Additional Secretary or Secretary. I had decided to retire from the State government. I was already promoted to the rank of Chief Secretary and posted as Special Chief Secretary and Chief Commissioner of Land Administration (CCLA), which is the second-highest civil service position. It is considered a stepping stone for appointment as Chief Secretary in Andhra Pradesh. I was quite aware that given my inflexible nature, I would not meet the job requirements of Chief Secretary. I was happy to retire as CCLA. However, at the suggestion of a few friends, I gave my consent for central deputation in December 2003.

At the end of February 2004, I received orders for posting as Secretary in the Ministry of Coal. This ministry was considered one of the lucrative ones. I believe there were many contenders who lobbied for it. I neither approached anyone, nor did I know the minister Ms

Mamata Banerjee, who might have had say in choosing the secretary for her ministry. However, rumours in Delhi were that two influential Andhra politicians may have helped me get the assignment: BJP leader Mr Venkaiah Naidu and Mr Chandrababu Naidu.

I joined the ministry in the second week of March 2004. Ms Mamata Banerjee was the Cabinet Minister and Mr Prahlad Singh of BJP was the Minister of State (MoS). Ms Banerjee was in Kolkata when I joined. I thought I could see her as soon as she returned to Delhi. However, she did not come to Delhi for more than a week. I received feelers that she was unhappy that the new secretary had not called on her after taking charge. I, therefore, decided to go to Kolkata to meet her. My meeting was fixed at her residence. Mr Shashi Kumar, acting Chairman Cum Managing Director (CMD), Coal India, accompanied me. I had heard about the spartan lifestyle of Ms Banerjee, but what I saw was simply unbelievable. It was a small house in a lower middle-class locality of Kolkata. We were ushered into a small room which had been partitioned with a curtain in the middle. It had a wooden cot with a cotton mattress and two plastic chairs. Ms Banerjee joined us in a few minutes and received us with warmth. There was no hint of annoyance at the delay in my formally calling on her.

After the exchange of pleasantries, I explained to her the need for an early decision on the appointment of a regular CMD for Coal India. The post was lying vacant for over nine months after the suspension of the previous CMD Mr NK Sharma. She heard me patiently but did not say anything. This was my first and last meeting with Ms Banerjee. Parliament elections were announced in early April and Ms Banerjee did not return to Delhi. She continued in Kolkata, canvassing for the elections. Her party, the Trinamool Congress (TMC), fared poorly and she was the lone TMC candidate elected. The National Democratic Alliance (NDA) also lost the election and Ms Banerjee ceased to be Minister of Coal. After she returned to Delhi, I sent word to her for a farewell meeting in the ministry. She declined.

Ms Banerjee had commendable simplicity and there is no doubt about her personal integrity. But she was not immune to misuse of her office for her party's interests. Soon after Ms Banerjee took charge of the ministry, she forced the acting CMD Mr Shashi Kumar to appoint 50-odd TMC workers as trainees. They were to be posted as securitymen at the coal mines of the North Eastern Coal Fields Limited. No procedure was followed in their selection: no advertisement, no tests and no interviews. A list of names was handed over to Mr Shashi Kumar and he was told to issue appointment orders. Mr Kumar told me none of these persons attended training. They used to simply mark their attendance and attend to Ms Banerjee's party work. There was already huge surplus and unproductive manpower in Coal India which was being reduced through a Voluntary Retirement Scheme (VRS). The government had banned new appointments in Coal India. But the ban was relaxed to facilitate recruitment of TMC workers. Ms Banerjee however, was not the only minister to have misused her office to employ her nominees in CIL. I was told that many other ministers in the past had done the same.

Ms Banerjee also laid the foundation stone in Kolkata for a super-speciality hospital to be set up by Coal India. The board had not approved such a proposal. She pressurised the CMD to pay ₹ 25 lakh to the Kolkata Municipal Corporation for eviction of squatters from the corporation land proposed for setting up the hospital. There was little justification for Coal India to set up a super-speciality hospital in Kolkata. First, Coal India is a mining company and it is not its business to run super-speciality hospitals. Second, Kolkata has less than 0.25 per cent of the Coal India work-force. If the hospital was meant to be a welfare measure for CIL workers, it should have been set up in Jharkhand where almost 50 per cent of Coal India's employees work. This did not matter to Ms Banerjee. She also pressurised the Coal India chairman to make large donations to several NGOs of her choice.

Before Ms Banerjee took over as minister, eminent persons were appointed as independent directors on the board of the Neyveli Lignite Corporation (NLC), a company under the Ministry of Coal. Ms Banerjee directed the then secretary to appoint some non-descript TMC workers as directors on the NLC board. It was pointed out to her that the directors were appointed for a fixed tenure and they had completed only a few months in office. But she ordered that their appointment be terminated to make place for her nominees. After Ms Banerjee ceased to be minister, the services of the TMC workers appointed to CIL were terminated after training. The proposal to set up the super-speciality hospital was dropped. The proposal to appoint her nominees on the NLC board automatically lapsed.

As is usually the case with the Government of India, Ms Banerjee did not assign important work to MoS Mr Singh. No files were therefore being submitted to the MoS. According to the Travelling Allowance Rules, the Personal

Assistant (PA) to MoS was not entitled to travel by air. In case of urgency, the Secretary's approval was required. While no files were being sent to the MoS, his PA was submitting TA bills every week—seeking approval of air travel for taking urgent files to Nagpur. I approved two visits but when he submitted the bill the third time, I asked for the list of urgent files he had to take to the MoS. Mr Singh was livid and recorded on file that the Secretary had no business to ask such questions; he should approve his PA's air travel. I had to tell Mr Singh that the clause of approval by the Secretary was included in the TA Rules to control wasteful expenditure.

Mr Singh's office used to routinely interfere in the commercial decisions of the coal companies. In my first meeting with the CMDs, I had to clarify that they were not bound to comply with communications emanating directly from the minister's office which they thought were not in the company's interest. They were free to write to me for guidance and instructions.

When I discussed these issues with service colleagues, they felt that it was better to allow direct interaction between the CMDs and the ministers. The CMDs were capable of handling these matters on their own. These minor issues should not be allowed to become a source of friction between a minister and a secretary. However, I think the Secretary of the ministry has the responsibility to intercede and support the CMDs if undue pressure was exerted on them.

12. Mr Shibu Soren Joins and Resigns: The Minister who Disappeared

With the General Election of 2004, the NDA government was defeated and the United Progressive Alliance (UPA) government was installed in Delhi. In May 2004 Mr Shibu Soren of the Jharkhand Mukti Morcha (JMM) took over as the Cabinet Minister in the Ministry of Coal. Mr Dasari Narayana Rao of the Congress party was appointed the Minister of State. Mr Soren brought Mr Pradeep Dixit as his Officer on Special Duty (OSD). Mr Dixit was a sophisticated, urbane and articulate person but had little knowledge of the working of the government. Mr Dasari Narayana Rao had a bright and experienced Private Secretary in Mr AA Rao.

On assumption of charge, I briefed both ministers about the work of the coal ministry and the issues that needed their immediate attention. There was serious shortage of coal in the country and a number of power plants had reached critical stock levels of coal. Coal supply had to be increased on an emergency basis. Coal India Ltd (CIL) was without a full-time regular CMD for almost nine months, which adversely affected its performance. Coal production suffered because of delays in environment and forest clearances and problems of land acquisition. Other issues that needed attention at the political level were the opening up of the coal sector for commercial mining, bringing transparency in allocation of coal blocks, and curbing the role of the mafia in coal marketing.

The ministers did not show any interest in these issues. Their interest was primarily in faster allocation of coal blocks, transfers of officials in coal companies, creating more employment in Coal India, and grant of coal linkage although no coal was available for new linkage. On each of these issues, my views were diametrically opposite to those of the ministers.

Within a few weeks of Mr Soren taking charge, a Jharkhand court issued an arrest warrant against him in an old murder case. Mr Soren went underground. Finally, he resigned as minister on the 24 July 2004.

13. Prime Minister takes Charge: Three Big Ticket Reforms

Prime Minister Dr Manmohan Singh assumed charge of the coal ministry after Mr Soren resigned. I thought it was an opportune time to push through reforms in coal sector. In early August, when I met the Prime Minister to brief him, I submitted three policy issues for his consideration. (1) Opening up the coal sector for commercial mining; (2) Allocation of coal blocks through competitive bidding; and (3) Marketing of coal through e-auction to non-core consumers.

Opening-up the Coal Sector for Commercial Mining

I submitted to the Prime Minister that Coal India alone could not meet the growing demand for coal in the country. It was necessary to open up the sector for commercial mining as early as possible. The Coal Mines (Nationalisation) Amendment Bill, to open up coal mining to the private sector without restriction of captive use, was pending with the Parliament since 2000. The Standing Committee recommended the Bill for adoption by an overwhelming majority with a dissent note only from the Left parties. The arguments of the Left parties and the CIL unions against opening up the coal sector for commercial mining were mere political posturing. They had no real merit. The reasons that prompted nationalisation of coal mines in the early 1970s—lack of financial and technical competence in the private sector and exploitation of labour—was no more valid in the changed economic environment. If captive mining by the private sector was accepted for over a decade, there was hardly any justification to stall the opening up of the coal sector for commercial mining.

I also explained to the Prime Minister that captive mining had inherent drawbacks. First, we were forcing industries that had no core competence in coal mining to get into a totally unrelated field. Second, by allowing coal mining for captive use by several medium-sized industries, we were fragmenting the industry and losing the advantage of scale of operation and modern technology. Third, we have no monitoring mechanism to ensure that the coal mined in captive mines is employed only for captive use. In a situation of scarcity, when there is huge premium in the market, coal from captive mines would inevitably get diverted to the black market, thus promoting corruption and black money. Fourth, the present system of allocation of captive blocks offers a huge advantage to industries that get coal blocks over those who are not able to get coal blocks. It is, therefore, discriminatory.

The Prime Minister agreed with my arguments. But he felt it would not be possible to get this amendment through the Cabinet because of strong resistance from the Left parties and the trade unions. This stance is unfortunate. The government went all out on issues like the Indo-US nuclear deal and FDI in retail, despite opposition from a large spectrum of political opinion. It did not show similar determination in opening up the coal sector for commercial mining where the resistance was only from Left parties and CIL unions. In the short and medium term, opening the coal sector for commercial mining was far more important for the country's economy than the Indo-US nuclear deal or FDI in retail. Had we opened up coal mining to the private sector for commercial mining, along with the power sector, in the early 1990s, we would by now have at least half a dozen large coal mining companies in the private sector. This is what happened in the telecom sector. The country would not be facing huge shortage of coal and large outgo of foreign exchange on the import of coal. If India has to meet its energy demand we need to have at least half a dozen coal companies, each producing over a 100 million tonnes of coal annually, and not 100 small companies producing 1 to 5 million tonnes of coal.

Allocation of Coal Blocks through Open Bids

My second suggestion to the Prime Minister was to change the system of allocation of coal blocks and introduce competitive bidding to bring transparency and equity in the process. The Prime Minister readily agreed to this suggestion and wanted an approach paper to be submitted.

E–Marketing of Coal

Another policy initiative I discussed with the Prime Minister during my briefing was the problem of large-scale black marketing of coal under the patronage of the coal mafia. I proposed to introduce e-marketing of coal initially for the non-core sector on an internet-based platform. Eventually, we would have about 25 per cent of coal produced by Coal

India on the spot and futures market. The Prime Minister agreed to take up e-marketing on an experimental basis in one company first and expand it to other companies after seeing the results of the first e-auction.

Coal is a major source of energy for India and will remain so in the foreseeable future. It is also a sector that is beset with serious problems of land acquisition, issues related to environment and forests, rehabilitation, labour relations, mafia operations and law and order. It is not as glamorous as the petroleum sector but is far more important for the country's energy security. It requires considerable political input for coordination with State governments, central ministries and trade unions. However, in terms of political leadership, coal has not received the attention and importance that it needs and deserves.

Many ministers have used the ministry for their own or their party's interests, instead of contributing to the sector. It was, therefore, a good opportunity to attempt reforms in the sector while the Prime Minister held the portfolio.

14. Allocation of Captive Coal Blocks: PMO and Ministers Scuttle Transparency

The process of allocation of coal blocks to the private sector for captive use had started in 1993, through a Screening Committee headed by the Coal Secretary. But information about coal blocks available for captive mining was not widely publicized. Geological reports about the blocks were considered confidential and not shared with the applicants. They had to get this information surreptitiously from the Central Mine Planning and Design Institute Limited (CMPDIL), one of Coal India's subsidiary companies. Between 1993 and 2002 only 15 blocks were allotted to private parties. This is an average of 1.5 blocks a year. There were a limited number of applicants for most blocks. As long as an applicant fulfilled the criteria for allocation, selection might not have posed serious problems for the Screening Committee. As the number of applicants per block started increasing, the ministry started to subdivide blocks into smaller sub-blocks. This was done without reference to geological or geographical features unmindful of the loss of coal at the barriers.

By the time I took charge of the ministry, the number of applicants for each block had increased considerably although still in single digits. I found a number of applicants fulfilling the criteria specified for allocation for each block on offer. This made objective selection extremely difficult. It was neither practical nor desirable to subdivide blocks into smaller sub-blocks to satisfy all eligible applicants. It was because of this dilemma that I thought of open bidding as a possible solution. This would eliminate subjective decision-making and also generate additional revenue for the State.

Coal blocks vary widely in geology and quality of coal. The cost of mining could vary from less than ₹ 300 a tonne in a good open cast mine to more than ₹ 2,000 a tonne in a deep underground mine. The quality of coal could vary from A-grade (>6200 K Cal/tonne of UHV) to G-grade (1300 K Cal/tonne of UHV). Apart from useful heat value (UHV), there are other characteristics that decide the commercial value of coal. Because of the large variation in cost and quality in different blocks, discretion in allocation left enormous scope for favouritism and corruption. In a situation as complex as this, it was impossible to take a fair and objective decision through the Screening Committee.

Geological reports with fairly accurate data about the extent of reserves and quality of coal were already available with the government. The CMPDIL had undertaken detailed exploration. I, therefore, thought that open bidding after making geological reports available to all prospective bidders would be a far more rational, objective, equitable and transparent system of allocation of coal blocks. Besides, by tapping part of the windfall profit, the auction method would also be fair to companies who did not get captive blocks and needed to source coal from CIL or imports.

Even before the Prime Minister took charge of the ministry, I had prepared a discussion paper and invited all stakeholders for an open house discussion in June 2004. This included industry associations like the Confederation of Indian Industry (CII), the Federation of Indian Chambers of Commerce and Industry (FICCI), the Federation of Indian Mineral Industries (FIMI), the Associated Chambers of Commerce and Industry of India (ASSOCHAM), etc. I also invited user ministries of the Government of India and representatives of all the companies whose applications were pending in the Ministry of Coal. Not many participants were enthusiastic about open bidding. Their main argument was that the cost of coal to be mined would go up if coal blocks were auctioned. This was irrational. Participants at open auctions are hard-headed businessmen with an acute sense of profitability. They do not make irrationally high bids. The price at which coal from CIL was available would automatically have put a cap on the bid amount. A production sharing arrangement for the entire life of the mine would have ensured that there was no immediate cash outflow. This would ensure that the project cost was not impacted. I think the industry resisted because they didn't want to pay for something that was hitherto available for free. To an extent, it was a reflection of corporate India's aversion to transparency.

Despite the reservations expressed at the stakeholders meeting, I prepared a policy note and submitted it to the MoS Mr Dasari Narayana Rao in mid-July.

The Screening Committee had no legal sanction. It was constituted by an administrative order. A change from the Screening Committee to a bidding system could have been implemented through another administrative order. However, to ensure that the proposed system was on sound legal footing, I sought the law department's advice on the legal framework for implementing open bidding. Simultaneously I asked the CMPDIL to prepare bid documents and evaluation criteria by engaging the services of a reputed international consultant so that the bidding process could start soon after Cabinet approval. To maximise competition, a list of blocks available for captive bidding was uploaded on the ministry's website and also publicised through newspaper advertisements. I was confident that the new system could be in place well before the end of the calendar year. I kept Screening Committee meetings on hold pending proposed changes in the procedure.

Mr Rao returned the file seeking clarifications. On the 30th July 2004 I replied to his queries and marked the file to the Prime Minister, who had by now taken over as Minister of Coal.

Prime Minister Approves Open Bidding

On the 20th August 2004 the Prime Minister approved allocation through open bidding. He wanted a Cabinet Note on this. After the Prime Minister's approval, we received a note from the Prime Minister's Office (PMO) enumerating the possible problems in moving to open bidding. It is understood that this note from the PMO was based on an unsigned note given by the MoS to the PMO. Simultaneously, a number of letters started pouring in from Members of Parliament opposing the proposed move towards the bidding system. This included one from Mr Naveen Jindal who had considerable interests in coal mining.

(*Courtesy:* Tehelka)

Law Ministry Suggests Amendment to Coal Mines Nationalisation Act

By early September 2004 the law ministry's opinion suggesting amendment to Section 3A and Section 34 of the Coal Mines Nationalisation Act was received. While submitting the Cabinet Note, I clarified the doubts raised in the PMO. I also suggested an ordinance be issued to make necessary legislative amendments. This would help begin the bidding system immediately and all pending applications could be decided through open bidding.

MoS Tries to Scuttle the Proposal

On the 4th October, while submitting the file to the Prime Minister, the MoS made the following noting:

"It is difficult to agree with the view that Screening

> Committee cannot ensure transparent decision-making. This alone was not adequate ground for switching over to a new mechanism, particularly when the interests of core infrastructure areas are involved.
>
> Proposal for competitive bidding may not be pursued any further, as it would invite further delay in allocation of blocks and considering that the Coal Mines (Nationalisation) Amendment Bill, envisaging competitive bidding as a selection process for allocation of blocks for commercial mining, was pending in the Rajya Sabha with stiff opposition from trade unions and others concerned."

This noting is important for two reasons. First, there was not even a remote connection between competitive bidding for allocation of captive blocks and the Coal Mines (Nationalisation) Amendment Bill pending in the Rajya Sabha. The opposition from trade unions was to opening the coal sector for commercial coal mining (by removing restriction of captive use), and not to introduction of open bidding for allocation of coal blocks. The MoS tried to create confusion and delay the process of decision-making by introducing such irrelevant issues. Second, Mr Shibu Soren later used this noting of the MoS to reverse the Prime Minister's decision to introduce open bidding.

Because of the confusion created by Mr Rao, a meeting was held in the PMO where it was decided that the change in policy should be prospective. All applications received up to the 28th June 2004, when the concept of open bidding was first made public, would be decided through the existing system of the Screening Committee. The PMO returned the file with the direction to amend the Cabinet Note to make the policy prospective. The PMO also wanted clarification on implications of the Coal Mines (Nationalisation) Amendment Bill, on the proposed bidding process. The PMO directed that there was no need to issue an ordinance to amend the CMN Act to give effect to the bidding process. A bill could be introduced in the forthcoming session of the Parliament.

I resubmitted the Cabinet Note with necessary clarifications and amendments to the MoS by December end, who marked it to Mr Shibu Soren who had by now returned as Minister of Coal.

The Prime Minister is Appraised

On the 17th January 2005 I met the Prime Minister to inform him that important files relating to the coal ministry were being deliberately delayed. I requested that he personally intervene. One of the issues that figured in this discussion was the introduction of competitive bidding for allocation of captive coal blocks. The Prime Minister called his Principal Secretary Mr TKA Nair and requested him to speak to the Minister of Coal. The same evening I sent a note to Mr Nair impressing upon him the urgency of approval of the Cabinet Note in order to bring necessary legislative amendments in the forthcoming budget session of Parliament.[11]

Mr Soren Kills the Proposal for Open Bidding

However, despite explaining the hurdles being created by Mr Rao and Mr Soren in my meeting with the Prime Minister, Mr Soren on the 25th February 2005 recorded following noting on the file:

---

11. Annexure 14-I.

> "It is seen that it has been categorically stated that the Prime Minister in his capacity as Minister of Coal and Mines has approved the proposal of the ministry to make allocation of coal blocks for captive mining on the basis of competitive bidding system. A perusal of Prime Minister's note recorded by Mr KV Pratap, Deputy Secretary, on page 14 N ante does not categorically speak of approval of the proposal. Rather he has directed that the matter be placed before the cabinet for consideration and decision. I have gone through the entire issue. As Minister of Coal, I am in complete agreement with the views expressed by MoS (Coal) in his note dt. the 4th October 2004 and as such, the proposal need not proceed further."

Mr Rao and Mr Soren joined forces to kill the proposal aimed at creating a transparent and objective method of allocation of coal blocks.

The Proposal is Revived

Mr Soren again resigned as Minister of Coal on the 1st March 2005 to take over as the Chief Minister of Jharkhand. The Prime Minister took charge of the ministry again. I revived the proposal and resubmitted the Cabinet Note for his approval on the 7th March clearly indicating that all applications received by the cut-off date of the 28th June 2004 would have been disposed of by June 2005. If immediate decision on introduction of the bidding procedure was not taken, pressure would again mount on the government to continue with the current procedure. The PM approved the draft Cabinet Note on the 24th March after which it was circulated to the user ministries and State governments for comments. After incorporating the comments received, the final note was resubmitted to the PM through the MoS on the 21st June for consideration of the Cabinet.

MoS Succeeds in Derailing the Proposal

While submitting the file to the Prime Minister, the MoS made the following comments:

> "The implications of such a decision by the Cabinet need to be considered in great detail and there was a general reluctance on the part of power utilities to participate in competitive bidding due to cost implications."

Open bidding would not have an impact on the price of power. It would, on the other hand, provide a level playing field between those who would get coal blocks and those who would have to procure coal from CIL. This was discussed in great detail, time and again. Raising the same issues repeatedly was meant to delay the introduction of the bidding process as much as possible, so that the old system of discretionary allocation could be continued. Regretfully, the MoS finally succeeded.

The Principal Secretary to the PM Mr Nair held a meeting on 25th July with the chief secretaries of the governments of coal-bearing states and secretaries of the user ministries of the union government. At this meeting I explained that the proposed bidding system is aimed at bringing transparency and objectivity. No change in the role of State governments and central ministries was envisaged. They would continue to provide inputs with regard to the bonafides and technical evaluation of applicants. The revenue generated from the auction was proposed to be put in a special fund to provide for social and physical infrastructure in coal mining areas. This would mitigate the adverse impact of mining on local communities. States should therefore welcome the proposed policy.

It was decided at this meeting that the Cabinet Note should again be amended to incorporate the concerns of the State governments where coal blocks were located. It was further decided that since amendment to the Coal Mines (Nationalisation) Act was likely to take considerable time, the Ministry of Coal would continue to allot coal blocks for captive mining through the Screening Committee until the new competitive bidding procedure became operational.

From this I concluded that there was no political will to proceed with the bidding route and the proposal had been put into cold storage. A bill for amendment to the Coal Mines (Nationalisation) Act to put the bidding system into operation had already been drafted in consultation with the law department. If political will existed, an amendment could have been brought about by issuing an ordinance.

Anyway, as desired by the PMO, the Cabinet Note was again modified incorporating the views expressed by representatives of State governments. The MoS kept the file with him; he was waiting for me to retire in December. Instead of submitting the file to the PM, seeking approval for placing the matter for a decision of the Cabinet, he returned the file on the 12th January 2006 with the following noting:

> "PMO had taken the view that the required amendment to CMN Act is a time-consuming exercise and has allowed the department to proceed with allocation of captive coal blocks under the extant mechanism. 20 coal

and lignite blocks are already put on offer and are under process and as such there is no immediacy in the matter."

After I left the ministry, the issue was further deflected by linking the bidding for coal blocks with the bidding process for all minerals by amending the Mines and Minerals (Development and Regulation) Act. Since this amendment was in the domain of another ministry, it ensured that the existing procedure could continue for a few more years.

It is clear from the sequence of events that neither the industry nor the political system wanted a transparent and objective procedure. Every possible effort was made to delay the introduction of open bidding until all the fully explored good blocks had been allocated.

I tried to bring in as much transparency and equity as possible after it was decided that allocation through the Screening Committee should continue within the limitations of a discretionary system. Wide publicity was given about the blocks available for allocation through newspaper advertisements and the ministry website. Complete geological reports were made available to all applicants at nominal printing cost, to enable them to evaluate the property before applying. Successful applicants were encouraged to form joint ventures for coal mining, to be fair to small consumers and accommodate as many eligible applicants as possible. Where it was not possible to form joint ventures, arrangements were made to select a lead partner who would mine and supply coal to associates.

With these changes in policy, it became possible to accommodate almost all eligible applicants. In the absence of open bidding, these were the next best options created so as to be as objective as possible.

15. In Defence of CAG: Why the Prime Minister is Wrong

The Comptroller and Auditor General of India (CAG), Mr Vinod Rai, did an excellent job of bringing the huge coal allocation scandal into the public domain. The defence put up by several ministers, and the Prime Minister's statement, in Parliament rings hollow and unconvincing. The statements given by Mr P Chidambaram and Mr Salman Khurshid, criticising the CAG, are so bereft of logic that they do not even merit comments. I would, however, like to address the statement made by the Prime Minister in Parliament.

1. About the Screening Committee

The CAG observed that the Screening Committee did not follow a transparent and objective method while making recommendations.

The Prime Minister claimed that allotments through the Screening Committee were based on the assessment of applicants on several parameters. The final judgment was of several participants acting collectively and hence there was no merit in the CAG's observations that the allotment process was not transparent and objective.

This argument strikes at the very root of the policy change that the PM had approved after being satisfied that the Screening Committee route was not objective and transparent. As long as the number of applicants were limited, such an arrangement could still meet the criteria of transparency and objectivity. According to the CAG's report, 108 applications were received for Rampia and Dip Side of Rampia Block. I found it difficult to make an objective selection when the number of applications was in single digits. How could the Screening Committee take objective decisions when the number of applicants per block had run into three digits? Even a joint decision of several participants acting collectively becomes suspect when the minutes of the meetings do not disclose the reasons for selecting or rejecting.

2. Role of the Audit

The Prime Minister stated that in a democracy it is difficult to accept the notion that a government decision to seek legislative amendment to implement a change in policy should come for adverse audit scrutiny. Policy-making is the business of the government and not that of the CAG.

Nowhere in his report has the CAG suggested or commented on what government policy should be. All that the CAG said was that on account of abnormal delay of more than eight years in implementing a policy that the government itself had formulated, there was an undue financial gain of about ₹ 1.86 lakh crore to private parties. This gain was obviously at the cost of the exchequer. If the CAG is not to comment on the loss caused to the exchequer, then whose business is it in a parliamentary democracy?

3. Abnormal Delay in Implementing Policy

The Prime Minister stated that the CAG's premise that competitive bidding could have been introduced in 2006 by amending existing administrative instructions is flawed and based on selective reading of the opinions given by the Department of Legal Affairs. Major coal and lignite bearing states like West Bengal, Chhattisgarh, Jharkhand, Odisha and Rajasthan, which were governed by opposition parties, were strongly opposed to a switch to competitive bidding. The issue was contentious and the proposed change to competitive bidding required consensus among various stakeholders with divergent views. This is inherent in the legislative process.

The fact is that if there was political will, open bidding could have been implemented in 2004. While claiming that there was resistance from opposition-governed states, and that the proposed change to competitive bidding required consensus, the Prime Minister made no mention of the concerted and repeated attempts of Mr Rao and Mr Soren to obstruct, sabotage and stall open bidding. Based on the opinion of the law department, a Bill to put the bidding process on sound legal footing was drafted in 2004. Needless and frequent references to the law department, and tossing of files raising irrelevant issues and objections, were made with the sole aim of delaying the implementation of proposed changes in policy.

In any case, when policy is internally sabotaged, who would convince opposition-governed states or build consensus. Coal Mines (Nationalisation) Act, 1973, a comprehensive legislation nationalising over 700 private coal mines and having far-reaching implications for the country's economy could be enacted within weeks of the government taking a decision. It took the present government less than three months to process an ordinance to protect convicted MPs, thus overturning a Supreme Court decision. It puts a big question mark on the government's sincerity in bringing about transparency when a minor amendment seeking procedural change in the method of coal block allocation takes several years.

4. Computation of Undue Gain

The Prime Minister stated that the CAG's computations on gain to private parties can be questioned on a number of technical points. First, computation of extractable reserves based on averages would not be correct. Second, the cost of coal production varies significantly from mine to mine even for CIL due to varying geo-mining conditions, method of extraction, surface features, number of settlements, availability of infrastructure, etc. Third, CIL has been generally mining coal in areas with better infrastructure and more favourable mining conditions, whereas the coal blocks offered for captive mining are generally located in areas with more difficult geological conditions. Fourth, a part of the gain would in any case be appropriated by the government through taxation and the Mines and Minerals (Development and Regulation) Bill, being considered by Parliament, under which 26 per cent of the profits earned on coal mining operations would have to be made available for local area development. Moreover, as the coal blocks were allocated to private companies only for captive purposes for specified enduse, it would not be appropriate to link the allocated blocks to the price of coal set by CIL.

There is no doubt that the extractable reserves and cost

of mining varies widely from mine to mine as does the quality and sale price. It is precisely for this reason that an average offers a representative value for broad assessment. While CIL might have relatively better properties, this advantage is more than offset by its large overheads and low productivity. The CAG's estimate cannot be faulted because part of the windfall gain would come back to the government by way of taxes. The fact that coal blocks were allocated to private companies only for captive purposes for specified enduse does not reduce their financial gain, as long as there is no control over the price of their output.

There are others, including financial experts, who have questioned the CAG's estimates on the grounds that the purported benefit has been worked out for the entire mining period but future gains have not been discounted to derive current value. This argument is not valid as the CAG has not arrived at his figures by summing up future cash flows. In a way, the CAG's method of computation represents Net Present Value (NPV) of the coal blocks allocated to private parties free of cost. For the reasons stated by the CAG in his report, these estimates are on the conservative side. This figure could be much more depending on the assumptions one makes. The CAG adopted average cost of mining and average sale price of CIL in its computation. One could argue that CIL's cost of mining is high, and private companies with better management and utilisation of mining machinery would have lower costs and hence much higher gain. Or, one could use the e-auction price or import price for computation, as these are the only options available to those who do not have linkage from CIL. In which case gain would increase further. The CAG's method of computation is fair and objective and is about the best that could be done from available data. Those who have criticised the CAG estimates, including the Prime Minister, have not offered a more scientific and rational method.

In a TV interview and subsequently in an article published in *TheTimes of India* dated the 28th August 2012, Mr Salman Khurshid, then Law Minister found fault with the CAG for not explaining how much of the ₹ 1.86 lakh crore the government would have got. The CAG is not a soothsayer. No one can predict what the government would have gained if the open bidding route had been adopted. The bid price would depend on several factors such as the quality of coal, market conditions, extent of competition, timing of bidding, the state of the economy at the time of bidding, and so on. For all one knows, in a booming economy, it could have been even more than the CAG's estimates. Even if it was 50 per cent of the CAG's estimate, it was a huge loss to the exchequer. The important point is not the actual figures of gain computed by the CAG, but the scale of fraud and lack of transparency and equity in continuing a system that provided an opportunity for corruption, rent-seeking and favouritism.

In another TV interview, Mr Naveen Jindal, Member of Parliament, argued that all over the world mining properties are given free and governments receive revenue by way of royalty and taxes. I am not aware of any country where fully explored mining properties are given free. What are being given free are virgin areas with minimal geological information where large amounts of money has to be sunk as risk capital in carrying out exploration, which may or may not result in commercially minable discovery. Even such properties in most countries are not given free.

There is usually a production-sharing arrangement when commercial production starts. We, in India, have been following this system while allocating hydrocarbon properties since the mid-1980s. In the US, federal coal properties are allocated through a bidding process after making an assessment of the Fair Market Value (FMV) since the early 1980s. A number of Indian companies that have acquired coal mining rights in Australia, Africa and Indonesia in recent years have made huge investments to acquire these properties. They would be required to pay royalty and all other taxes applicable under the local law in addition to the upfront capital investment.

Defending the government in a TV interview to *News X* TV channel, the Minister of Coal Mr Sriprakash Jaiswal claimed that no pulls or pressures were involved in the allocation of coal blocks. He also claimed that no coal blocks were allocated during his tenure. I do not know how the minister knew that no pressures or pulls were exerted when no coal blocks were allotted during his tenure. It is naïve to say that no pressure was exerted when thousands of crores of rupees worth of resources were up for grabs. Pressures come in the form of enticements such as post-retirement assignments, partnership in business, bribery, blackmail or pure intimidation. Pressures also come from friends and relations. I encountered all of them. I am sure many other actors in the process of allocation have also encountered similar pressures. Some can resist these pressures. Others succumb.

However, it must be said to the credit of the Prime Minister that at no time did the PMO make recommendations or exert pressure in favour of any party. Even in the case of Hindalco, where the CBI has decided to register an FIR, the request was only to re-examine the case on merit.

Mr Vinod Rai and his reports on the 2G scam and Coalgate have been often criticised as over-activism. They have been held responsible for the economic slowdown in the country. People from within the establishment and well-meaning intellectuals have taken such a view. There is no doubt that 2G and Coalgate have significantly contributed to the economic slowdown and policy paralysis. However, it is wrong to blame Mr Rai. He did not go beyond his assigned constitutional responsibility. His estimates of undue gain to private companies was not wide off the mark at the relevant point of time. His reports have clearly brought to focus how wrong policies can be adopted, perpetuated and exploited for wrongful gain.

It is unfortunate that while the Prime Minister was keen on implementing open bidding, he was unable to counter vested interests within his government and party. The government's inability to take a right decision at the right time has resulted in Coalgate and subsequent CBI investigations monitored by the Supreme Court. To save its skin, the government has resorted to hasty and arbitrary cancellation of allocations. All this has resulted in policy paralysis. It has also led to enormous amount of litigation and unproductive work for the courts, the Central and State governments and private companies. This litigation will further delay production of coal from captive blocks and force the country to import more coal and add to inflationary pressures and worsen the already adverse trade balance.

16. E–Marketing of Coal: Ministers Dump Prime Minister's Policy

The problem of large scale black marketing of coal was another policy initiative that was discussed with the Prime Minister at my briefing meeting. Despite its large resource base, India always suffered from shortage of coal. This shortage generated a thriving black market and a powerful coal mafia, patronised by the political system. A large number of bogus industries were registered only for allotment of coal that could be sold in the black market. A number of genuine industries and brick kilns that had no coal linkage had no option but to procure their requirement of coal from the black market. There were several mafia dons operating in concert with officers of Coal India. They purchased coal release orders from the bogus industries and sold them at high premium to the actual users. This racket has continued for decades and was accepted in the industry as *fait accompli*.

At the root of this racket is an unscientific and faulty pricing policy where demand and supply do not determine the price. It was not possible to change the system overnight. I, therefore, thought of making a beginning by marketing coal to non-core consumers through e–auction. A few industries got coal at cheaper notified prices while others procured it in the black market at a high premium.

The best quality of coal was available with Eastern Coalfields Limited (ECL) and Bharat Coking Coal Limited (BCCL), the two eastern subsidiaries of CIL. While coal mafia earned hefty premium these companies were making huge losses and were referred as sick companies to the Board for Industrial and Financial Reconstruction (BIFR).

At an informal meeting when I proposed e-marketing of coal, only Mr Partho Bhattacharya, the CMD of BCCL who later became the CMD of CIL, agreed to take up test marketing. Other CMDs were very sceptical, almost reluctant to even experiment. A platform for e-marketing was already available with MSTC Ltd, a Government of India company, and Metal Junction, a joint venture of Steel Authority of India Limited (SAIL) and Tata Steel.

The Prime Minister had agreed in principle when I briefed him in July 2004. I now submitted a formal note for his approval. The Prime Minister approved test marketing of a small quantity of 1.6 lakh tonnes. The first test marketing was organised at BCCL in November 2004. It was a great success. Many coal consumers participated. The BCCL received additional revenue of about ₹ 1.5 crore for a small quantity of 1.32 lakh tonnes of coal.

Mr Soren Stops the E-Auction

With the resounding success of this experiment, I submitted a note to extend e-auction to all coal companies through the MoS Mr Rao, to Mr Soren who had returned as Minister of Coal. The success of the first e-auction had rattled the coal mafia and they were up in arms against extension of e-auction to all coal companies. The MoS kept the file with him for over a month. While submitting the file to Mr Soren after a month, the MoS made the following noting:

> "In view of the issues involved, the Minister of Coal may like to take a detailed presentation for further consideration."

Mr Soren did not take a presentation but before he resigned as coal minister to take over as the Chief Minister of Jharkhand, he ordered that no further e-auction be conducted. A proposal to bring transparency in coal marketing was thus nipped in the bud.

While the file for extending e-auction to other coal companies was under submission to the ministers, I received a telegram from Gauhati saying that on every rake of coal dispatched from North Eastern Coal Limited (NECL), the coal mafia collected a premium of ₹ 5 lakh. Coal produced in the NE Coal Ltd was of high calorific value although slightly higher in sulphur content. This coal was in great demand from the brick kilns of UP and Bihar. While the NE Coal Ltd was making huge losses, the coal mafia was making a killing. In anticipation of approval to extend e-marketing to all coal companies, I advised the Chairman, Coal India to sell the entire coal of NE Coal Ltd only through e–marketing. The results were far beyond our imagination. On every rake sold, Coal India received a premium of ₹ 25 lakh over and above the notified price. This raised the hope that these perennially loss-making coal companies could turn around.

Mr Soren took serious exception to my advice to the Chairman, Coal India to market coal from NECL by e-auction. He complained to the Prime Minister accusing me of insubordination.

Prime Minister Approves E-Auction in All Coal Companies

I was able to get approval to extend e-auction to all coal companies only after Mr Soren resigned a second time to become the Chief Minister of Jharkhand and the Prime Minister took charge of the ministry. By the time Mr Soren returned to the ministry a third time, e-auction was on a firm footing. Mr Soren could not undo it.

I had thought of e-auction as the first step towards creating a robust spot and futures market for coal. The idea was to put about 25 per cent of Coal India's production on the market through e-auction for proper price discovery. I also wanted an integrated and transparent coal market where imported and indigenous coal could be traded on calorific value and other quality parameters. Unfortunately, e-auction did not move beyond the first stage and coal pricing remains subjective, arbitrary and in a state of confusion.

17. Appointment of the CMD, Coal India: Blackmail by the Ministers

When Mr Karia Munda was the Minister of Coal, the then Chairman of Coal India, Mr NK Sharma, was kept under suspension following complaints of irregularities in the procurement of capital equipment and explosives for Coal India. By the time I joined the ministry, Mr Sharma was under suspension for about nine months and Mr Shashi Kumar, Director (Marketing), was holding additional charge. There was serious coal shortage and almost all power plants in the country had reached critical stock levels (less than 15 days requirement). Quite a few had reached super critical levels (less than 7 days requirement). Operations of Coal India were suffering in the absence of a regular full-time CMD.

To appoint a full-time CMD, a proposal to create a supernumerary post in the rank of CMD had been sent to the Department of Personnel and Training (DOPT)—with the approval of Ms Mamata Banerjee. With the change in government, the DOPT wanted fresh approval from the new minister. I briefed Mr Soren about the proposal. After his approval communication was sent to the DOPT for early creation of the supernumerary post. Soon thereafter, Mr Soren received a letter from Mr Tek Lal Mahto, MP, seeking the reinstatement of Mr Sharma. Now Mr Soren wanted to reinstate Mr Sharma by recalling the proposal while an inquiry against him was still pending. I advised Mr Soren that such a flip-flop may damage his credibility. He agreed with my suggestion but later, in a complaint to the Prime Minister, he alleged that I had obtained his signature on the file by misleading him. I was told that a fat sum was offered to Mr Soren on behalf of Mr Sharma.

Finally, after the Prime Minister took charge of the ministry, the government approved the creation of a supernumerary post in the grade of CMD. Interviews for the post were held on the 15th September 2004. The Public Enterprises Selection Board (PESB) recommended two officers in order of merit, the first being acting CMD Mr Shashi Kumar. Ever since they joined, Mr Soren and Mr Dasari Narayana Rao had pestered Mr Kumar for monthly payments which he resisted. Just before the interview, an approach was made to him on behalf of the MoS who wanted a onetime payment of ₹ 50 lakh and a monthly payment of ₹ 10 lakh to appoint Mr Kumar as the regular CMD. Mr Shashi Kumar refused.

Mr Rao Initiates Action against Mr Kumar

After the mandatory vigilance clearance from the Central Vigilance Commission (CVC), the file on Mr Kumar's appointment was submitted to Mr Rao on the 15th October. Mr Rao returned the file on the 29th, seeking investigation against Mr Kumar for his alleged role in the procurement of explosives for Coal India.

PESB and CVC Recommendations are Rejected

Following the doubts expressed by the MoS on the integrity of Mr Kumar, a further report was sought from the Chief Vigilance Officer (CVO) of Coal India. The CVC was again consulted on Mr Kumar's vigilance clearance. The CVC said there was no case against Mr Kumar, after which the file was resubmitted on the 24th December for his appointment as CMD. By this time Mr Soren, was re-inducted as Minister of Coal. The private secretaries of the two ministers met Mr Kumar over dinner to convince him to agree to the ministers' demands. At the minimum, they suggested that he become a channelising agent for funds to be received from CMDs of CIL subsidiaries. They told him that all past Coal India CMDs had paid ministers, and there was nothing unusual about it. Once again, Mr Kumar refused.

The MoS recorded a long note and finally took a view that the CVC's advice in the matter was not acceptable and the matter needed to be processed further overlooking name of Mr Kumar. Mr Soren approved the noting of the MoS and the file was returned to me.

I resubmitted the file after further clarification on all issues raised by the ministers, bringing it to their notice the PESB is an independent institution created to select Directors and CMDs of PSUs. The CVC is the highest authority in the country on vigilance matters of public servants. Based on the available records, there was no valid reason to reject the recommendations of the PESB and the CVC in respect of Mr Kumar. I requested the ministers to reconsider the matter. The MoS reiterated his views and recommended the rejection of Mr Kumar. Mr Soren, as the cabinet minister approved.

I had failed to persuade the ministers to see reason. I had no option but to send the entire record with my opinion, and the opinion of the ministers, to the Department of Personnel and Training (DOPT) for placing the matter before the Appointments Committee of the Cabinet (ACC) for a final decision.

Ministers Call for My Explanation

The Ministers took serious umbrage to my referring the case to the ACC. I was called the next day to explain why the second name in the panel was not proposed for consideration and how the proposal could be sent to the DOPT when the minister had already rejected recommendation of the PESB. The ministers wanted the proposal of the second person on the panel to be processed. Perhaps they wanted to start a round of negotiations with him. I had to remind the ministers that, according to the Business Rules of the Government of India, only ACC was empowered to accept or reject PESB recommendations. The Minister of Coal was only one member of the Committee. The other members of the Committee, i.e., the Home Minister and the Prime Minister also have to consider the matter before the PESB recommendation could be rejected. The secretary of a department is responsible for compliance with Business Rules. Therefore, I was duty bound to send the entire record for the consideration of the other members of the ACC, although the Minister of Coal did not agree with the PESB recommendations.[12]

ACC Approves the Appointment of Mr Kumar

Meanwhile, Mr Soren resigned again to take over as the Chief Minister of Jharkhand. The Prime Minister then approved the appointment of Mr Shashi Kumar as Coal India CMD, overruling the opinion of Mr Rao and Mr Soren. The Prime Minister could do so because Mr Soren had resigned. I doubt if this would have been possible if Mr Soren was minister.

The ministers constantly put pressure on Mr Shashi Kumar. At times, they humiliated and intimidated him for not meeting their demands. Mr Kumar exhibited exemplary courage and fortitude, rare in Coal India executives, in resisting the illicit demands of the ministers. He was willing to forgo his legitimate claim to the position of CMD, CIL, rather than succumb to their blackmail.

This was not an isolated instance of demands made by ministers to approve appointments at the board level in coal PSUs. There were many officers in CIL subsidiaries who were more than willing to make monetary and other

12. Annexure 17-I.

contributions and enjoy ministerial protection for their misdeeds. I understand that this is a common practice in central PSUs and also in a few government departments. I was therefore, not surprised when the nephew of Mr Pawan Bansal, the then Minister of Railways, was caught red-handed accepting a bribe for the appointment of Mr Mahesh Kumar as Member, Railway Board. There are many public relations agencies of industrial houses in the country that are willing to make payments on behalf of incumbent officers, in return for favours to be extracted after they are appointed. How can chiefs of central public sector undertakings and heads of the government departments control corruption in their organisations if they have to bribe ministers for their appointments? This rot at the top level of the political executive is a major cause of institutionalized corruption in the country. It has become so brazen that the Chief Minister of Andhra Pradesh, Mr Kiran Kumar Reddy, while addressing probationers of the All India and Central Services recently, had no qualms in advising them not to worry about political corruption as the money made by politicians is anyway returned to the people during elections. What a fall in the political standards of the country!

18. Games that Members of Parliament Play

Soon after I took charge of the ministry I met the CMDs, to work out a strategy to deal with coal shortage. One of the suggestions was to outsource small and shallow deposits by open bids to private contractors. These are deposits with lifespan of two to five years. Coal India Limited (CIL) had surplus workers but moving them from one area to another was virtually impossible because of trade union pressure. Besides, it was not considered worthwhile for CIL to invest in small equipment for these deposits with limited mine life. Private contractors, on the other hand, would be able to use the equipment in other civil works at the end of the contract period. Accordingly, small areas in Bharat Coking Coal Limited (BCCL) and Central Coalfields Limited (CCL) were given on contract to private agencies.

One morning, soon after the work on these mines started, I got a call from Mr Chandra Shekhar Dubey (CS), Congress Member of Parliament from Dhanbad. Mr Dubey was member of the Parliamentary Standing Committee on Coal. Our conversation was somewhat like this (translated from Hindi):

CS: "Mr Secretary, how could you order outsourcing of coal in BCCL without my permission?"

Me: "Mr Dubey, the Board of Directors takes decisions in these matters in the best interests of the company. The ministry has no role."

CS: "No, I am told it was your decision."

Me: "No, it was CIL's decision with which I concurred."

CS: "But how could they take such a decision without my knowledge. I am the Member of Parliament of the area."

Me: "Mr Dubey, it is a management decision of the company. Why should they consult the MP of the area? I have also headed public sector companies at the state level. I never consulted the MP or the MLA of the area on how to run my company."

CS: "That may be so in your Andhra Pradesh. It does not happen in our Jharkhand. I want you to stop this outsourcing immediately. Otherwise I will stop it."

True to his words, the supporters of Mr Dubey laid siege to the mine the next day and stopped work. Mr Bhattacharya CMD, BCCL called to inform me that Mr Dubey's supporters were not allowing workers of the contractor to enter the mine. I called the Chief Secretary of Jharkhand Mr Sharma and requested him to direct the District Magistrate to ensure that the contractor is allowed to work. The next day Mr Dubey called me again to say that he had stopped the work and there is no use calling the Chief Secretary in these matters. No Chief Secretary or District Magistrate could remove his protesting workers, he said. Soon enough, I realised that in Jharkhand no civil servant howsoever senior, could take on the coal mafia. Because of Mr Dubey's intransigence, work at the mine remained suspended for a couple of weeks and a large quantity of coking coal was destroyed in spontaneous fires.

I recalled my days as Collector in Andhra Pradesh. In a similar situation the District Magistrate would have had a free hand to deal with the matter. Here, even the Chief Secretary was not able to ensure that action is taken under the law against a recalcitrant Member of Parliament.

A number of houses belonging to BCCL were in illegal occupation of squatters for a long time. The squatters were not only in illegal occupation of company property, they also enjoyed other perks available to BCCL employees such as free power, water, etc. The BCCL was not able to evict these squatters due to political patronage and fear of the coal mafia. After Mr Dubey was elected MP, he too wanted a BCCL house to be allotted to him. Mr Bhattacharya declined his request. This infuriated Mr Dubey. He started to insult Mr Bhattacharya and issue statements in the press levelling false allegations against him. Mr Dubey now became the main patron of the squatters. He used his goons and did not allow even enumeration, let alone eviction, of the illegal occupants. The letter the CMD wrote to me about the activities of Mr Dubey and his illegitimate demands indicate how Members of Parliament consider themselves above the law.[13]

The inability of the government to enforce law and order has enabled elected representatives at all levels to meddle in contract management. This is across the board, from the Panchayat level to Parliament. They meddle in work of government, PSEs and even private companies.

13. Annexure 18-I.

They have all become rent-seekers; they contribute significantly to crime and a parallel economy. It is almost impossible for a Collector or Superintendent of Police to survive in Dhanbad without compromising with the coal mafia and its political patrons. After retirement, on one of my visits to Dhanbad in connection with an inquiry into an underground mine accident, I learned that Mr Dubey was on the warpath with the District Magistrate. One day he locked the DM's office chambers in the collectorate. This was a criminal act for which he should have been prosecuted. Instead, the Collector was transferred. Unlike past chief ministers who stood by officers, one cannot expect the likes of Mr Madhu Koda to stand by the District Magistrate or Superintendent of Police who is willing to take on the coal mafia.

The first successful e-auction of coal in BCCL had rattled the coal mafia. If extended to all coal companies, it had the potential to make a serious dent in the illicit income of the political patrons of the mafia. Soon, efforts started, to move me out of the coal ministry. Mr Dubey fired the first salvo. He was annoyed with me because of my support to the BCCL CMD in his efforts to clean up company operations. In early November, Mr Dubey wrote to the Prime Minister alleging that I had Swiss Bank accounts and had visited Switzerland to update my transactions. Mr Dubey wanted the CBI or a committee of parliament to investigate my alleged misdeeds.[14]

In my response to Mr Dubey's letter,[15] I requested the Cabinet Secretary to institute an inquiry through the CBI or

14. Annexure 18-II.
15. Annexure 18-III.

any other agency and if the allegations were found false, Mr Dubey should be made to suffer the legal consequences of maligning the reputation of a senior civil servant. I also requested that the conduct of Mr Dubey, in making baseless allegations, should be brought to the notice of the Speaker for such action as deemed fit. Mr Dubey's letter was followed by a similar letter to the Coal Minister, Mr Soren, by another Member of Parliament, Mr Giridhari Yadav.

Mr Dubey and Mr Giridhari Yadav are not isolated instances of blackmail of civil servants and executives of public sector companies by Members of Parliament. Many MPs make unreasonable demands, and then make false allegations to harass honest officers. Mr Narendra Kumar Kushwaha of the cash-for-query infamy was one such MP. This BSP MP shamelessly demanded money from the then CMD of Northern Coal Fields Limited and when refused complained against him. I wrote to the Cabinet Secretary for suitable action to stop such blackmail.[16] By another letter I also brought this MP's extortion bid to the notice of the Central Vigilance Commission (CVC) who in response, suggested that the CVC be made the focal point to examine all complaints against officers who come within its purview. No independent action should be initiated against an officer without the CVC first examining the complaint.[17] As advised by the CVC, I wrote to the Cabinet Secretary seeking an institutional mechanism to ensure that Members of Parliament do not misuse their privileged position to blackmail senior officers. I suggested a meeting of the

16. Annexure 18-IV.
17. Annexure 18-V.

Committee of Secretaries be called to find a solution.[18] However, no such meeting could take place until I retired.

In another instance, Mr Furkan Ansari, Member of Parliament, wanted Mr RP Ritolia, CMD of Central Coalfields Limited (CCL), to hire about 100 Muslims of Jamtara area. When the CMD refused, a false complaint was made to the Prime Minister by Mr Ansari and Mr Dubey. The PMO made discreet enquires and found the complaint to be false. The PMO advised me to inform Mr Ansari suitably.[19]

It is not just ordinary Members of Parliament who indulge in such reprehensible behaviour. Those entrusted with higher responsibilities such as chairmen of parliamentary committees also at times show scant respect to senior executives of PSEs, and speak to them in intemperate and insulting language. One such instance was that of Mr Ananth Kumar, Chairman of the Standing Committee on Coal and Steel. Without listening to what CIL CMD had to say about a transfer recommended by him, Mr Ananth Kumar snapped at the CMD in the following words:

> "Such behaviour from the CIL CMD and MCL CMD will not be tolerated. My party (the BJP) would see to it that the CIL CMD and MCL CMD realise their mistake and understand the value of political leadership. The CMD would regret the day when Mr Saha's request was not acceded to. In the remaining ten months (of Mr Shashi Kumar's tenure as CIL CMD), I would teach him a lesson so that he would repent."

18. Annexure 18-VI.
19. Annexure 18-VII.

Mr Kumar's letter to me vividly brings out how senior political leaders seek favours and misbehave with executives of PSEs.[20]

Mr Ananth Kumar, who was a minister in the past, forgot that civil servants and executives of PSEs applying political pressure to further their service interests, breach the Conduct Rules. By insisting on retention of Mr Saha at Kolkata he was abating his misconduct. He also forgot that as Chairman of the Parliamentary Standing Committee, the least that was expected of him was civilised and courteous behaviour. He perhaps thought that as Chairman of the Standing Committee, he had a right to order, bully and threaten the CIL CMD with dire consequences if his orders were not complied with. I sent a note to the PM through the MoS Coal, seeking appropriate action against Mr Ananth Kumar.[21] I do not know if the MoS sent the note to the Prime Minister.

Following the second resignation of Mr Soren, e-auction of coal was extended to all coal companies after the Prime Minister's approval. After e-auction notification was issued in Mahanadi Coalfields Ltd (MCL), Mr Dharmendra Pradhan, BJP MP who represented Talcher area of MCL, approached me for sale of coal to some non-core consumers at notified price. I informed him that no exception could be made once a notification was issued for sale of coal through e-auction. Mr Pradhan was apparently not happy. E-auction had seriously reduced the flow of black money in the coal belt. The MPs targeted the CIL Chairman and me. They used the ministry's Parliamentary Consultative Committee

20. Annexure 18-VIII.
21. Annexure 18-IX.

to vent their anger. At a consultative committee meet in early August, Mr Pradhan got nasty. He made extremely insulting and derogatory remarks against me. The MoS, who presided over the meeting, allowed Pradhan to continue with his tirade, instead of reprimanding him.

After working tirelessly to reform the coal sector in the face of heavy odds and stiff resistance from within and outside, these compliments from a Member of Parliament were too much for me to digest. I decided to quit. The next working day I sent my request for voluntary retirement with immediate effect.[22] In my letter to the Cabinet Secretary Mr BK Chaturvedi I wrote:

> "The conduct of Mr Dharmendra Pradhan, Hon'ble Member of Parliament from Orissa at the Consultative Committee meeting of the Ministry of Coal on Friday, 5th August 2005, leaves me in little doubt that we have descended to such low levels of working in our parliamentary democracy that it is becoming increasingly difficult for civil servants to work with self-respect, dignity and professional integrity.
>
> I find it impossible to function in such a vicious environment and would like to be immediately relieved of my responsibilities as Secretary (Coal). This letter may be taken as my request for voluntary retirement. Pending approval of my request, I am proceeding on earned leave with effect from the 9th August 2005."

On 17th August 2005 I met the Prime Minister for a farewell call. I wanted to express my concern at the insult and humiliation that Members of Parliament heap on civil

22. Annexure 18-X.

servants and senior executives of PSUs. I asked the Prime Minister if Members of Parliament behaved as they did with Secretaries to the Government of India, what would they behave with young District Collectors. How can officers in districts function in a fair and impartial manner if they are subjected to blackmail and intimidation by elected representatives. The Prime Minister expressed anguish and stated that he faced similar problems every day. But it would not be in the national interest if he was to offer his resignation on every such issue. I do not know if the country would have got a better Prime Minister if Dr Manmohan Singh had resigned, instead of facing the humiliation of his own ministers not implementing or even reversing his decisions. By continuing to head a government in which he had little political authority, his image has been seriously dented by 2G and Coalgate although he has had a spotless record of personal integrity.

While offering no solution, the Prime Minister expressed full confidence in me and assured me of his full support. He advised me not to press for premature retirement and continue in office till the date of my superannuation. At his advice I resumed duty on 22nd August 2005.[23] However, it became clear to me that there was little chance of lasting reform in the coal sector with the limitations within which the Prime Minister functioned.

Soon after the ugly incident in the Consultative Committee meeting, Mr Pradhan wrote to the Prime Minister justifying his misconduct.[24] The Prime Minister's Office asked for my remarks, which were sent by a coal

23. Annexure 18-XI.
24. Annexure 18-XII.

ministry memorandum.[25] This communication is self-explanatory. It indicates how ignorant, vengeful and intemperate our elected representatives can be. Mr Pradhan found fault with me for not censoring the presentation made by the CIL Chairman. He did not know that a Consultative Committee of Parliament is meant for free and frank deliberations and every officer has full freedom of expression. They need not be constrained by views of a secretary or a minister. In his defence, Mr Pradhan invoked the Nehruvian model of democratic socialism which neither he nor his party (BJP) had anything to do with. He thought that any opinion against this model, which the country has given up long ago, is sacrilegious. On the issue of R&R policy, Mr Pradhan deliberately misinterpreted my statement to justify his outburst. He thought these excuses gave him a license to insult a senior civil servant. MPs and MLAs should understand that the Constitution gives them the privileged position to uphold the dignity of the House. By their misconduct and misbehaviour, they damage their own image and that of the House they represent.

25. Annexure 18-XIII.

19. Mr Shibu Soren: The Minister with a Personal Agenda

After Mr Soren took charge of the ministry, in keeping with the general practice in Government of India, he assigned virtually no work to the MoS Mr Dasari Narayana Rao. Understandably Mr Rao was unhappy. When he mentioned it to me, I suggested he speak to either the Prime Minister or the Congress President who could advise Mr Soren suitably.

Mr Soren comes from the heartland of the coal mafia and was obviously well aware of the extent of corruption in the coal industry. He was, however, not shrewd enough to exploit this on his own. Since his Officer on Special Duty (OSD) Mr Dixit also had no experience of the working of the government, Mr Soren needed a cooperative Secretary and chief of CIL. Unfortunately for him, both were unwilling to cooperate. Initially, efforts were made to browbeat CIL chief Mr Shashi Kumar into submission. Mr Soren took serious objection to Mr Kumar addressing the press on coal price revision without his permission. He wanted Mr Kumar to be suspended for insubordination. I explained to Mr Soren that the CIL Chairman did not need his permission to speak to the press. In any case, it did not warrant suspension. Wiser counsel prevailed and Mr Soren did not press further.

After a couple of weeks, work distribution was revised. All ministry files would now be routed through the MoS, Mr Rao. I do not know what prompted Mr Soren's change of heart. Whatever the reason, Mr Rao ably assisted Mr Soren in scuttling every effort to bring transparency in the coal sector.

Transfers of Directors in CIL Subsidiaries

The potential to make money is not uniform in all CIL subsidiaries. Directors were more than willing to pay an asking price for more lucrative postings. Transfer of directors from one company to another was, therefore, a lucrative business for coal ministers. To stop this scandal, the NDA government banned ministers from transferring directors. All such proposals had to be submitted to the ACC for approval. Mr Soren made verbal requests for inter-company transfer of directors. I explained to him that the directors were appointed for a fixed tenure of five years, and it is neither in the interest of the companies nor the officers to make inter-company transfers unless there were compelling reasons to do so. He did not like this. When I did not comply with his oral directions, Mr Soren sent a formal note seeking the transfer of a director from the CMPDIL to BCCL. I informed him that he did not have the authority for such transfer and that the proposal would have to be sent to the ACC. I advised him to speak to the Prime Minister informally before sending the proposal on file, as it would be embarrassing if the ACC rejected a cabinet minister's proposal. He insisted on the proposal being sent to the ACC. The ACC rejected it after Mr Soren resigned.

Efforts to Seek My Transfer

Apparently the coal ministers found me totally uncooperative. They began to take steps to get me out of the ministry. Members of Parliament were instigated to make false complaints against Mr Kumar and me.

Mr Chandra Shekhar Dubey, the Dhanbad MP, came to my office seeking allocation of coal blocks for two companies. During this meeting, I asked Mr Dubey how he had made a complaint against me to the Prime Minister that did not have an iota of truth. Mr Dubey was candid. He told me the complaint was drafted in the office of the MoS and he was asked to sign it. Since he was angry with me on issues of outsourcing and housing in BCCL, he signed the complaint.

Unlike many Members of Parliament who make requests while seeking favours, Mr Dubey was used to giving orders. In his inimitable style he ordered me to allot coal blocks to two of his nominees. I informed him that the two companies he proposed for allocation were not eligible under the existing guidelines. They could not be considered. Mr Dubey became angry. He said he knew how blocks were allotted in the past and if I do not accede to his request, he would make my remaining tenure in the ministry miserable. I told him to go ahead.

Both Mr Rao and Mr Soren were unhappy with my stand on coal block allocation, coal marketing through e-auction, appointment of the CIL CMD, and long-term coal linkage. After his return as minister a second time, Mr Soren invited me for a one-on-one meeting. Our conversation in Hindi was somewhat like this:

Mr Soren: Secretary Saheb, if there is no understanding between you and me, how will the ministry function? People outside think you run the ministry and not me.

Me: Sir, as secretary and minister we have distinctly assigned roles in the Business Rules of the Government of India. It is my responsibility to advise you on what I consider in public interest. It is your right as minister to accept or reject my advice. I will sincerely implement any order that you may issue in writing, even when it is against my advice.

Mr Soren: Because of your support, the CIL CMD does not comply with my orders.

Me: As minister, you are not expected to interfere in the day to day working of CIL. The CIL Board is expected to manage its business and not the government. However, the government is empowered to direct CIL on policy matters. The CIL Board and Chairman are bound to comply with written orders.

Mr Soren: However, all orders cannot be given in writing.

Me: No officer of the government or CIL is bound to comply with oral orders, if in his judgment such orders are not in public interest.

Mr Soren: But with such an attitude it is very difficult to work.

Me: But Sir, this is how I have worked all my life and I cannot change my way of working. But I assure you I would never give you wrong advice. I will sincerely comply with all your written orders.

Mr Soren was not pleased with this conversation. He decided it was time to get me out. He wrote to the Prime Minister requesting my transfer and also to initiate administrative action for insubordination and failure to follow the Business Rules.[26] He also informed the PM that I was an appointee of Mr Chandrababu Naidu during the NDA government and I could work to create a rift in the UPA. He buttressed his case by claiming I did not care for him because he was an Adivasi minister. The government asked for my comments. I sent my reply to the Cabinet Secretary by my letter dated 22nd March 2005.[27] In my covering letter to the Cabinet Secretary I wrote:

> "There is no gainsaying that I have had difference of opinion with both the Minister of State and the Cabinet Minister on several issues of policy and administration.
>
> In my understanding I have performed my duties in the manner that is expected of a member of the Civil Service. As Secretary to the Government, I am deeply conscious that I cannot effectively discharge my responsibilities without full political support from my ministers. However, I am at loss to understand as to what can be done."

On 2nd March 2005 whispersinthecorridors.com, a website on civil service gossip, commented:

> **Will Coal Secretary be Repatriated?**
>
> Bureaucratic circles are agog with reports that Secretary, Coal, Prakash Chandra Parakh, is being repatriated to the parent Andhra Pradesh cadre. 1969 batch Andhra

26. Annexure 19-I.
27. Annexure 19-II.

Pradesh cadre IAS officer, Parakh is considered to be an upright officer.

Mr Soren resigned on 1st March 2005 to take over as the Chief Minister of Jharkhand. Had Mr Soren continued as minister, the Prime Minister might have had no choice but to relieve me from the ministry. The five members of Mr Soren's Jharkhand Mukti Morcha were crucial for the survival of the UPA government. The Prime Minister has limited options in the fractured polity of our country as the survival of the government depends on the support of multiple small parties.

The minister's letter and my reply to the Cabinet Secretary raise fundamental questions about the role of the civil service. Democracy works on the basis of checks and balances. The founders of the Indian Constitution conceived a permanent and neutral civil service with constitutional guarantee against arbitrary action, as part of this scheme of checks and balances. While there is no question about the supremacy of the political executive in a democracy, the role assigned to the civil service is to keep a check on arbitrary exercise of political authority. This has to be understood and respected. It is for this that we need a strong institutional mechanism which clearly defines the role of the political executive and the civil service, and promotes mutual respect.

I am grateful to the Prime Minister for his confidence. With the pressure from Mr Soren, Mr Rao and Members of Parliament from the coal belt, it would not have been easy for the Prime Minister to support me. He ensured that I not only continue in the coal ministry but also persuaded me to complete my tenure after the unfortunate Dharmendra Pradhan episode.

I was not able to introduce competitive bidding for coal blocks, but internet-based e-marketing of coal was put on a firm footing although the ministers resisted strongly. I left the ministry with the satisfaction that each of the CIL subsidiaries, including the chronically loss-making BCCL, recorded operating profit. All power plants had adequate coal stocks; there was not a single power plant with critical coal stocks in December 2005 when I demitted office.

20. Supreme Court, CBI and Coalgate: Looking in Wrong Place

There was a flurry of activity after the CAG report on coal block allocation was published. PILs were filed too. The Supreme Court then directed the Central Bureau of Investigation (CBI) to investigate the allocation of coal blocks from 1993, when the Coal Mines Nationalisation Act was amended to permit captive mining in the private sector. The Supreme Court is monitoring the investigation. Allocations between 1993 and 2003 were made under a policy formulated by the government headed by the Congress party and continued by the following NDA government. In my opinion there is no case for investigation into allocations made from 1993 to 2003. The CAG has not made adverse observations on these allocations. Nor has anyone else complained against these allocations. No meaningful investigation can be made and responsibility fixed in cases that were decided decades earlier. This would only result in the frittering away of limited CBI resources in terms of manpower and expertise. It can at best amount to a witch-hunt.

The CBI is not equipped to find the truth. Its expertise lies in fixing and unfixing people. Unfortunately, it is doing so even in the Coalgate investigation although the Supreme Court is monitoring it. The CBI is almost totally staffed with police officers who have little or no exposure to policy formulation and its implementation. The entire investigation is in the hands of officers at the level of inspectors who have little understanding of the decision-making process in the government. When the CBI called me to Delhi, given the importance of the case and its economic and political ramifications, I expected that either the CBI Director or an officer one or two levels below him would interact with me. Certainly not inspectors of police who do not understand the difference between a coal block and a coal mine. In the two days I spent with the CBI, I explained in detail the working of the Screening Committee and the responsibilities of a secretary and a minister in decision making under the Business Rules of the Government of India. The allocation of Talabira II block also figured in these interactions. I explained the rationale of including Hindalco in this block, while modifying the Screening Committee recommendation. Their basic argument was that this change benefited Hindalco. I said, "Of course it has benefited Hindalco, just as allocation of other blocks has benefited hundreds of other private companies." It was precisely for this reason that I had proposed open bidding for allocation of coal blocks. They insisted that this change was because of pressure from the Prime Minister's Office (PMO). I categorically stated there was no pressure from the PMO, and that the case was considered entirely on merit. I said I take full responsibility for what I recommended. I thought the CBI had understood the logic of this decision.

I was surprised at the CBI's naiveté when they registered

an FIR in this case and a team of a dozen officers landed at my door to search my flat eight years after I retired. I did not understand what they expected to find in my house. Neither did they. While I took it in my stride, my wife was shocked and traumatised at this reward for 36 years of honest, sincere and dedicated service.

To my mind the entire approach of the CBI in investigating the coal scam is faulty. The CAG's report that prompted these investigations underlines the fact that unduly long delay in switching over to a transparent bidding system led to the coal scam. I had proposed the change in early 2004 and vigorously pursued it until I retired. The CBI has made no effort to elicit the reasons for this abnormal delay. Was this delay deliberate or otherwise? If deliberate, who was responsible for it? Did those responsible for this delay derive any advantage by continuing with the old discretionary system? If an ordinance to protect criminals, by reversing a Supreme Court order, could be processed in less than three months, why did a minor amendment which could have brought transparency and equity in allocation of coal blocks take so long? This is the crux of the matter that the CBI needs to investigate.

But the CBI is not doing that. Instead, it is involved in the meaningless exercise of examining thousands of documents of various ministries of the Central government, State governments and private companies to discover criminality where none may exist. I have no information about the facts of the 16 FIRs it has filed in Coalgate and cannot comment about the CBI's bonafides in these cases. However, about Talabira II coal block, in which the CBI has registered an FIR against Mr Kumar Mangalam Birla and me, I can say without hesitation that the CBI is either outright incompetent or is playing a deeper game which I do not understand. What can be more absurd than the CBI questioning the bonafides of Mr Naveen Patnaik, merely because he made a recommendation in favour of Hindalco? If a chief minister is not to canvass for projects he thinks would generate employment and revenue for his state, what is he Chief Minister for? With this kind of investigation, after wasting thousands of crores of public money, Coalgate may also end in a whimper like Bofors. The actual culprits responsible for the delay in the introduction of a transparent system, and those who benefited from the delay, could go scot-free.

Talabira II and Hindalco

Talabira II and Talabira III are sub-blocks of a contiguous coal block that has no geographical or geological features warranting its division into two separate mines. This division was unscientific and was done many years ago when coal blocks were identified for allocation to private companies for captive use. While Talabira III was with the Mahanadi Coal Fields Limited (MCL), a subsidiary of Coal India, Talabira II was identified for captive allocation. Such artificial division of coal blocks leads to loss of sizable quantity of coal at the barriers. Being a Mining Geologist myself, after I joined the ministry I directed that in future the boundaries of all coal blocks should be determined only by geological and geographical features. No blocks should be artificially subdivided.

Hindalco and Neyveli Lignite Corporation (NLC) were strong contenders for Talabira II. Both had equally strong credentials on the basic qualifying criteria of financial and technical competence and a credible downstream project. Hindalco was the prior applicant and the Government of Odisha strongly supported its case. Since the Ministry of Coal and the CBI have denied me access to relevant records, I do not recall the power ministry's views. However, the Screening Committee could have recommended allocation of the entire Talabira II block to Hindalco based on the recommendations of the State government and because it was the first applicant. The captive mining policy was essentially designed to get private investment in coal mining. On this ground alone the NLC's application for Talabira II could have been rejected. As a government company, the NLC could have been given a coal block outside the captive list. Thus, even if the whole of Talabira II was given to Hindalco, the CBI could not have accused me of abuse of office or corruption.

The Screening Committee did not have powers to decide allocation of coal blocks. It was a forum for inter-ministerial consultation where all stakeholders presented their case. All views were recorded and the Chairman took a final view. Screening Committee recommendations were examined in the Ministry and the coal minister decided on allocation. If the Screening Committee, for some reason, errs in its recommendation, the minister can and should take a decision that is fair and objective.

At the Screening Committee meeting, the following considerations were at the back of my mind for preferring NLC, in spite of the State government's strong recommendation of Hindalco:

1. NLC was the coal ministry's own company, which was sitting over a pile of surplus funds without new projects in hand. Allocation of this block would have opened up immediate avenues for profitable investment of NLC surplus funds.
2. Allocation of Talabira II to Hindalco would have meant development of Talabira II and III as two separate mines, and a loss of about 30 million tonnes coal in barriers.
3. Since MCL and NLC were both companies under the Ministry of Coal, it would be easy to persuade them to make a joint venture to develop both blocks as a single large mine, to take advantage of scale of operations and modern technology.

Based on the recommendations of the Screening Committee, a proposal for allocation of Talabira II to NLC was submitted to the Prime Minister as the Minister of Coal. While the Prime Minister's Office (PMO) was considering it, Mr Kumar Mangalam Birla made a representation to the Prime Minister contending that the Screening Committee had erred in rejecting their claim for Talabira II block. Mr Birla requested the matter to be reconsidered in the interests of justice. The

Chief Minister of Odisha also wrote to the Prime Minister, seeking reconsideration of the matter and allocation of this block to Hindalco. He was against the allocation of the coal block to NLC, which according to him would export power to other states and leave behind pollution in Odisha. His clear preference was for Hindalco, which he felt would add value within Odisha and generate additional employment and revenue. The PMO returned the file to the coal ministry along with these two communications for re-examination of the proposal.

Mr Kumar Mangalam Birla met me in my office and made a similar representation. He argued that rejecting Hindalco's claim merely because NLC was a government company was unfair, particularly when the captive mining policy was designed to seek private investment in coal mining. He also explained that the linkage earlier given for the project could not be used, because of the State government's delay in granting the mining lease for Bauxite. Because of the shortage of coal, CIL was in no position to honour the old linkage. While appreciating Mr Birla's argument I informed him that even if we reconsider the case, in the interest of conservation of coal, we would not agree to have Talabira II as an independent mine. Hindalco would have to join the proposed joint venture as a minor partner. After initial hesitation, Hindalco agreed to join as minor partner in the proposed joint venture.

After examining Mr Birla's representation and the Odisha Chief Minister's letter, I felt there was merit in their arguments and the case deserves reconsideration. Accordingly, after taking note of all facts, I made a recommendation that I felt was fair and just to all parties without compromising the prime concern of not splitting Talabira II and III into two separate mines. If I recall correctly, I had made two alternative proposals. Finally the Prime Minister approved the proposal to jointly allocate Talabira II to NLC and Hindalco, in his capacity as Minister of Coal. It was also decided to create a joint venture with all three companies holding equity in proportion to their share of coal.

The CBI has concluded there was conspiracy and corruption, because my revised proposal was at variance with the Screening Committee recommendation. As I have said previously, the Screening Committee was a forum for inter-ministerial consultation and did not have powers to make allocations. I was privy to Screening Committee deliberations, and was fully aware of the views of all stakeholders. It was, therefore, not necessary for me to get back to the Screening Committee while re-examining the matter in the light of representations received from the PMO.

I am not a legal expert; my knowledge of law is limited to what was taught during our training at the Academy when we joined as members of the Indian Administrative Service. Mr Ranjit Sinha, CBI Director, having been a police officer all his life and having the benefit of expert legal advice within his organisation, is far more qualified in the interpretation of criminal law. But I have a few questions for him with regard to the FIR registered against me.

1. Mr Birla met the Prime Minister and me to make a representation against perceived injustice done to his company. Does a citizen who makes a representation against a government decision which he considers unfair, automatically become a conspirator and criminal in the eyes of the law? Is there any evidence against Mr Birla that made the CBI conclude he

hatched a conspiracy along with me? If so, what is it?

2. Is there a law or rule which prevents a civil servant from re-examining a matter where a citizen feels that injustice has been done to him? Was Hindalco a bogus company? Did it not have financial or technical competence or a credible downstream project to qualify for allocation of this coal block? Was the claim of Hindalco on Talabira II inferior to that of NLC on merit? Is the CBI aware that Hindalco's project, for which the block was allotted, has been commissioned, whereas NLC shelved its power project? Does re-examining a matter by a civil servant, based on the representation of an aggrieved party, by itself amounts to conspiracy and corruption? Where was the abuse of power in this case?
3. Where did the CBI get the information that Talabira II was reserved for allocation to public sector companies? If it was reserved for the public sector, how could Hindalco apply for it? Why then did this matter come to the Screening Committee? The Screening Committee had no role in the allocation of coal blocks reserved for the public sector. Did the CBI publicise this false information merely to malign my reputation?
4. Where did the CBI get the information that the NLC had to shelve the project on account of reduction in its share of coal from Talabira II? Is the CBI aware that the NLC shelved the project because it became unviable after the Odisha government demanded 30 per cent power free? Why did the CBI make a false statement to the media?
5. Why did the CBI not consider it necessary to examine relevant files of the PMO as part of its

preliminary inquiry, before concluding that there was conspiracy and corruption?

6. Is the CBI aware that according to the Business Rules of the Government of India, unless powers are delegated to him, a Secretary only makes a recommendation? The minister takes the decision. Did the CBI not notice during its preliminary inquiry that the decision in this case was taken by the Prime Minister? If the CBI smelled conspiracy and corruption, why did it not name the Prime Minister in its FIR?
7. Did the CBI have any information about my role in the allocation of coal blocks to Visa Power and Navbharat Power? If so, what? And if not, why did the CBI go public with these totally irrelevant and baseless allegations?
8. Why did the CBI search my house? What was it expecting to get from this search, eight years after I retired? Is it not undue intrusion into the privacy of a citizen?
9. If the allocation of Talabira II to Hindalco was undue favour, why were all the 200 coal blocks allocated to various private companies not considered undue favour? Why was everyone else involved in these decisions not charged with conspiracy and corruption?

Through my career, my credibility with colleagues and those who worked with me has always been high. Sometimes, even those whom I never met or worked with have expressed appreciation for my sincerity and honesty. One such person was Mr Sudhir Mungantiwar, a former cabinet minister of Maharashtra. In a letter dated 24th September 2005 (translated into English), while I was Secretary in the ministry, he wrote:

> "I have never personally met you but I have heard a lot about you and your integrity. Hence, I am writing this letter to express my feelings about you. You are bringing changes in the system. I have heard many people praising your integrity. You started e-auction. The work you are doing, without being influenced by any political pressures, is indeed praiseworthy. I wish you all the best in your efforts to convert the loss-making Coal India into a profitable company.
>
> The Path of Truth you are travelling on is indeed praiseworthy. Truth sometimes frustrates, but it can never be defeated. My heartfelt best wishes to you."

In the midst of constant fights with my ministers and MPs, this letter from a stranger was a great morale-booster. Coming from a politician, this also indicates that despite all round degeneration in our political system, there is still a class of political leaders who value honesty and neutrality of civil servants.

After the CBI registered an FIR against me, I received overwhelming support from colleagues, persons from various walks of life, and service associations, not only of All India Services but also of other Central and State Services. Some of this communication has deeply touched my heart. I wish to quote from a letter I received from a former colleague with whom I worked in my first job with the National Mineral Development Corporation (NMDC), almost half a century ago. After he learnt of the FIR registered by the CBI, he wrote:

> "Hearty congrats for making the PM own responsibility in the Hindalco issue and proving beyond doubt how frivolous the CBI charges are.
>
> I admire and appreciate the courage you demonstrated in a highly polluted atmosphere of corruption. Your TV interviews are brief and brilliant and are to the point.
>
> The overwhelming support you received from one and all speaks volumes of your integrity. Mr Parakh, I must say with all humility at my command, if you are corrupt God is also corrupt. Bravo. Truth prevails."

In various TV debates that followed the registration of the FIR, despite the deep political divide, no political party accused me of corruption. The Prime Minister clarified that he took the decision based on the facts placed before him, and that it was an appropriate decision. But when the CBI registers an FIR it is bound to create doubts and suspicion in the minds of ordinary people, particularly when the full facts are not in the public domain. This is all the more so in an atmosphere of widespread corruption, where every government decision is suspect.

One does not expect the premier investigating agency of the country to build its case on falsehoods, half-truths and conjectures. I wish Mr Sinha had done his homework carefully before accusing me of conspiracy and corruption. He ought to have perused relevant files of the Ministry of Coal to understand the efforts I made to bring transparency, not only in the ministry but in the entire coal industry. It was all very well for him to tell the media that if no evidence is found, the FIR would be closed. But does he appreciate the irretrievable damage he has caused to my reputation, earned over a lifetime?

I have not abused my office, Mr Sinha. You have—by accusing Mr Kumar Mangalam Birla and me of conspiracy and corruption. My recommendations were well within the boundaries of the declared government policy. But you have acted without proper understanding of facts, rules and laws. Perhaps to impress the Supreme Court and the people at large of your newfound freedom from the 'cage'.

Since the Supreme Court is monitoring this case, as the custodian of fundamental rights of citizens, it has a duty to ensure that the CBI does not malign the reputation of citizens because its lacks professionalism and competence. The Civil Service and industry associations have widely condemned the CBI in this case. The court should direct, as a matter of principle, that the CBI should not go public with its investigations unless a case has reached the stage of filing a charge-sheet. This would ensure that the CBI does not indulge in character assassination of citizens in future.

Autonomy of the CBI

There has been considerable public debate on the autonomy of the CBI after the Supreme Court said that it was a 'caged parrot'. The measure of autonomy available to a member of the All India Service is commensurate with his or her will to exercise it. It is needless to blame the statute for lack of will. As long as an officer does not aspire for a post-retirement job, or has no fear of transfer, he has full autonomy to function according to his judgment.

As a member of the Indian Police Service, the CBI Director has full autonomy to function according to the dictates of his conscience. There was no compulsion on Mr Ranjit Sinha to show his progress report on Coalgate investigations to the law minister to 'correct his use of English'. This is what

earned the CBI the epithet of 'caged parrot'. If Mr Sinha was convinced that the Hindalco allocation was a conspiracy and had he the courage of conviction, he ought to have named the Prime Minister in the FIR.

No amount of statutory safeguards can make the CBI more autonomous as long as the persons heading it have a different agenda and are unwilling to exercise their autonomy. There is no doubt that the provision of 'prior sanction of competent authority' for prosecution under the Prevention of Corruption Act has been widely abused by the political system, to protect corrupt politicians and civil servants. However, blanket authority to the CBI to initiate criminal action without supervision and accountability would be a remedy far worse than the disease. It can become a serious threat to the economy and polity of the nation. The court and Parliament need to be aware of this pitfall when they decide on the autonomy of the CBI.

Part Three

Code for the Future

21. Civil Service, Ministers and People's Representatives

The relationship between the civil service, elected representatives, and the political executive is critical to the governance of India. Questions about this fundamental relationship came up in Mr Soren's letter to the Prime Minister seeking my transfer, and my response to that letter. It also emerged in the series of communications I exchanged with the Cabinet Secretary on the conduct of Members of Parliament *vis-a-vis* civil servants and CEOs of PSUs. This was not limited only to the coal ministry at the Centre. Similar issues cropped up from time to time even while I worked with the State Government. I have enumerated these in Part I of the book where I look at my stint with a State government. Over the years, the relationship between the civil service and elected representatives has deteriorated and become either adversarial or collusive. It ought to be harmonious and cooperative. This erosion has been the main contributor to poor governance of the country. If we want to improve the quality of governance, we have to create and nurture institutions that help create a healthy and cooperative environment in which the political executive, elected representatives and civil servants function in the overall interest of the country, and not to further personal and partisan interests.

Irrespective of its nature—democratic, socialist, capitalist, autocratic or imperialist—the only tool available to the state to implement its policies is its civil service. The efficiency, commitment, honesty and discipline of the civil service will determine the efficacy of governance.

Three tenets of the civil service were laid down for the British Civil Service in the 1854 Northcote-Trevelyan report. Since the architects of the Indian Constitution had largely drawn from the British Constitution, the same principles govern the civil services in India.

(i) **Permanence:** Civil servants do not change when ministers or governments change. They bring stability and continuity, allowing new ministers to take up office easily; the process of governance is disrupted as little as possible. Permanent civil servants also become experts in the fields of decision-making and departmental working.

(ii) **Neutrality:** Permanence makes this necessary. Civil servants must be politically impartial if they are to stay in office, while governments change.

(iii) **Anonymity:** Politicians are elected and must, therefore, take the decisions. They must also take the credit or blame for the policies. Civil servants must remain anonymous in the sense that they should not be held publicly accountable for their advice or for policy.

In a democratic form of government that India is, the most important determinant of administrative efficiency is harmony and understanding between the ministers and the civil servants. Civil servants should accept the supremacy of the political executive, just as representatives of people and politicians should understand that civil servants have to function within the framework of statutes, rules and regulations. These rules need to be applied uniformly to all citizens of the country, irrespective of their political affiliation. Mutual understanding and trust between the political executive and civil servants sets the tone for good governance. This relationship is delicate but has continuously deteriorated after independence. It was seriously dented during the Internal Emergency of 1975 and has reached a breaking point in the era of coalition governments.

Debate in the Constituent Assembly

In post-independent India Sardar Patel set the tone for relations between the political executive and the civil service. While replying to a debate in the Constituent Assembly on articles relating to the civil services, Patel said:

> "An efficient, disciplined and contented service assured of its prospects as a result of diligent and honest work is *sine qua non* of sound administration under a democratic regime even more than under authoritarian rule. The service must be above party and we should ensure that political considerations either in its recruitment or in its discipline are reduced to the minimum if not eliminated altogether.
>
> Today my secretary can write a note opposed to my views. I have given that freedom to all my secretaries. I have told them, "If you do not give your honest opinion for fear that it will displease your minister, then you

better go. I will bring another Secretary. I will never be displeased over a frank expression of opinion. Many of them with whom I have worked, I have no hesitation in saying that they are as patriotic, as loyal, and as sincere as myself. These people are the instruments of governance. Remove them and I see nothing but a picture of chaos all over the country.

As a man of experience, I tell you, do not quarrel with the instruments which you want to work with. It is a bad workman who quarrels with his instruments. So once and for all decide whether you want the service or not."

Requirement for Harmonious Relationship

This speech by Sardar Patel laid down four cardinal principles of a harmonious relationship between a minister and his secretary. These principles have been enumerated by the Hota Committee on Civil Service reforms, as follows:

1. Both minister and civil servant should perform their roles in accordance with the laws and the Constitution, as even a minor transgression can ultimately be subversive of good governance and the rule of law.
2. There should be trust and mutual respect between the minister and the civil servant as without unity of action at the highest level of the government, good governance is impossible.
3. Preservation of integrity, fearlessness and independence of civil servant is an essential condition of sound parliamentary system of governance. One of the important functions of a civil servant is to "speak truth to power".

4. Formation of government policy is the legitimate task of the minister. A civil servant must give his free and frank advice. Once the policy has been decided, it is the duty of the civil servant to carry out the policy diligently and faithfully, irrespective of his own views in the matter.

Civil Service on the Eve of Independence

Commenting on the quality of civil services in post-independent India, Paul Appleby said, "India shared with Britain the distinction of having the best body of generalist civil servants in the world." In contrast, Hong Kong-based *Political and Economic Risk Consultancy,* in a report released in 2012, ranked and rated the Indian bureaucracy as the worst in Asia, with a score of 9.21 out of 10.

Thus, on the eve of independence, India was fortunate to have an efficient, honest and fearless civil service and a highly respected and competent political leadership, with an exemplary record of great sacrifices in winning freedom for the country. But we have failed to build on these strengths.

Degeneration in the Political System

Degeneration in the political system started rather early after independence. Reading from a letter from a Congressman, at his prayer meeting, Mahatma Gandhi said:

> "This rot in the Congress is that of people's representatives in the legislative bodies of provinces. They are vociferous about stopping the widespread corruption, but they themselves resort to worse corruption. They take money from people to get licenses, indulge in black-marketing, trade in ignorance of masses,

corrupt the source of justice, and force administrative machinery to get transfers of administrative personnel."

Weeks before his assassination, the Mahatma read from another letter from a friend, Konda Venkatappaiah:

"Several MLAs and MLCs are following the policy of 'make hay while the sun shines', making money by the use of influence, even to the extent of obstructing administration of justice in criminal courts. Even the District Collector and other revenue officials are not free to discharge their duties on account of frequent interference by MLAs on behalf of their partisans. A strict and honest officer cannot hold his position, for false reports are carried against him to the ministers, who easily lend their ears to those unprincipled self-seekers."

Partisan interference in day-to-day administration and harassment of honest and straightforward officers, which has now become endemic, thus started soon after independence.

Degeneration in the Civil Service

The civil service stood its ground for some time, but could not do so for long as even the celebrated steel frame of the ICS started to giveway. In an article, CS Chandra, ICS, then Secretary, Rehabilitation, Government of India, wrote:

"A marked decline in the morale of the service became apparent in the early years of independence. Sardar Patel, who was in-charge of the home portfolio, was the one man who defended the service, whenever it was attacked inside and outside Parliament. His exit from the political stage was the death knell of the ICS whose decline now became quite evident. Interference in the

> day-to-day administration became frequent; ICS officers who yielded to political pressure were promoted over the heads of their seniors, whereas those who resisted such pressures fell out of favour. A new class amongst the ICS sprang up. Instead of devoting time and energy to work entrusted to them, their sole aim was to please their ministers. The weaker member of the service began to realise that it was not hard and conscientious work that was the passport to promotion, but sycophancy. Senior members of the service, in order to secure extension after superannuating or to get other lucrative appointments after retirement, were only too ready to carry out the behest of the ministers even when they found such requests to be contrary to the dictates of their conscience. Far more serious was another factor, which I call intellectual dishonesty. Some members of the service were clever enough to find out which way the minds of their ministers were working. They would record notes contrary to the dictates of their conscience to ingratiate themselves to the ministers."

A number of Commissions appointed during the Nehru era spoke about corruption and favouritism in high places and consequent demoralisation of the civil services.

The Khanna Commission that inquired into the misconduct of Chief Ministers and ministers of Orissa made following observations:

> "The officials cannot be oblivious of the fact that their promotion and future prospects are dependent on the goodwill of ministers. Being human, how many officials are prepared to jeopardise future prospects in order to

promote public interest? Quite a number of them with streaks of martyrs or high sense of duty would no doubt be prepared to take personal risk for the sake of public good, but there would also be a substantial number who would consider discretion to be the better part of valour. There would be quite a few unscrupulous officials who would try to prove more loyal than the king and on their own, go out of the way to secure a pecuniary advantage to the minister at the cost of public interest, in order to curry favour with the minister."

The Aiyar Commission inquiring into the misconduct of Bihar ministers made following observations:

> "It is undoubtedly the duty of the officers to carry out truly and faithfully the orders of the ministers, but at the same time it is also their duty to advise them clearly and firmly whenever the actions of ministers are not in accordance with the well-recognised and established principles of administration. Nothing can be more disastrous to the state than that the heads of administration should, instead of advising the minister properly, take to humouring them and toeing their lines. If the government undermines the morale of its officials, the executive arm of government itself will be weakened and if this thing goes for any length of time, the entire administration may become paralysed and thus wholly ineffective."

Nehru did not give the same support to the civil services that Patel gave. Nehru considered the civil service an impediment to the development of the country and often publicly criticised civil servants. Nehru also exhibited exceptional tolerance to corruption in high places. Lack of political support from the Prime Minister and growing political corruption started demoralising the civil services. Nehru, who had both the stature and ability to nurture civil service ethos and control political corruption, unfortunately did not pay adequate attention to these issues.

Internal Emergency and Civil Service

The Internal Emergency of 1975 made a serious dent on every organ of the state, including parliament, judiciary and the civil service. Instead of commitment to the core values of civil service—honesty, objectivity and fearlessness—Emergency demanded commitment and loyalty to individuals or the ruling party. A number of officers who stuck to the rulebook were persecuted and humiliated. Mr Mangal Bihari, a senior IAS officer of Rajasthan cadre, writes about the ill-treatment he received for not abiding by political dictates:

> "However, the flashpoint in the anger of the politicians at the Centre arrived in the mid-1970s when a big rally was organised in Delhi. Various states neighbouring Delhi were allotted quota of crowds to be brought to Delhi. Rajasthan also had a quota. Out of that, 10,000 were allotted to be drawn from among the workers of the Electricity Board. One cabinet minister was overall in-charge of organising the dispatch of men from Rajasthan.
>
> June is the month of storms and breakdown of electricity in Rajasthan, when trucks and men are required to be rushed to different places for immediate repairs. Therefore, it was inadvisable to allow so many trucks and men to be sent out to Delhi for a purely political exercise. I could not agree to these arrangements.
>
> At the rally, attendance from Rajasthan was less than

> expected, for which the blame was put on the Chairman, Rajasthan Electricity Board (the author). I was immediately transferred from the chairmanship of RSEB. A senior CBI officer was dispatched from Delhi to book me for any corruption mismanagement or inefficiency that may be located or fished out in my working. In a quick turn of events the Central Government had instructed the State Government to dismiss me from service. The massage was received by the then Chief Minister on telephone. He immediately recorded it and sent the note to the Chief Secretary for compliance."

How arbitrary and casual the decision-making process became even at the level of Chief Ministers is explained by Mr TSR Subramanian, former Cabinet Secretary, in his memoirs.

> "One evening around 5 PM that winter, TN Dhar, Secretary to the Chief Minister, telephoned me from Delhi and said that the Chief Minister has decided to replace the current Chief Secretary and that Kripa Narayan Srivastav should be the new Chief Secretary. Apparently Sanjay Gandhi had just dictated the instructions to the Chief Minister. I understood later from the grapevine that Col. Anand, the father-in-law of Sanjay Gandhi, was Garrison Commander in Goa at the time when Srivastav was posted as Chief Secretary there, and that this was almost the circuit utilised for eliciting the *firman* (a royal edict) from Sanjay Gandhi."

On how the civil service behaved after the Emergency, he writes:

> "With a new government of a totally different complexion in place, the order of the day was to condemn all

> Emergency excesses. Turncoats galore surfaced in the administration. Officers, who were enthusiastic henchmen of the erstwhile Emergency administration, suddenly wore the garb of implacable opposition and contempt for Emergency excesses. Who said civil servants were rigid and inflexible? When their own interests are involved they can put a chameleon to shame."

Current State of the Civil Service

There has been no looking up from the days of the Emergency. Transfers and postings have been extensively used all over India to make the civil service subservient to politicians and to cover-up corruption and maladministration. The position of the Chief Secretary and Cabinet Secretary, who head the civil services at the State and Central government respectively, has been seriously compromised by unceremoniously transferring holders of these offices and by selecting pliable and at times even known corrupt officers for these positions. The most brazen have been the appointments of successive chief secretaries in Uttar Pradesh who faced serious charges of corruption and who had to be removed from office on court orders.

Lamenting the sad state of India's civil services, the National Commission on Working of Constitution records:

> "Arbitrary and questionable methods of appointments, promotions and transfers of officers by political superiors also led to corrosion of moral basis of its independence. It has strengthened the temptation in the services to collusive practices with the politicians to avoid inconvenience of transfers and for officers to gain advantage by ingratiating themselves to political

> masters. They will do a politician's bidding rather than adhere to rules. Lest the situation should become more vicious, it is necessary that a better arrangement be conceived under the Constitution."

While the deterioration in civil service started even when the Congress party was in power at the centre and most states, the advent of coalition governments with short lives hastened the downward slide. Bimal Jalan writes:

> "Politicisation of bureaucracy in India is primarily the result of governments with short tenures pursuing their private or party interest in the guise of promoting public good. Any party which comes to power tends to appoint pliable bureaucrats who are expected to carry out the wishes of party leaders, irrespective of their merit or legality. If a bureaucrat does not comply, he is likely to be transferred to another position. According to one study, in one year alone, in Uttar Pradesh there were 1,000 transfers of elite IAS and IPS officers. Under one head of government, transfers ran at the average of seven per day. Under a second head of government that took office after expiry of six months, transfers rose to sixteen per day. Thus, over half the corps of IAS officers was transferred within twelve months of posting."

As a result of almost six decades of degeneration in the political and civil service systems, there are three types of officers in civil service today. First, those branded as loyal to a political party or leader; second, those who like chameleons are willing to switch loyalty to whoever is in power; and a small third category of officers who, despite all odds, still stand by the values of integrity and neutrality.

Ministers, MPs and MLAs do not like officers in the

third category and blackmail and harass them, or they are simply marginalised by giving them unimportant assignments. There is no institutional mechanism to protect civil servants from such harassment. If officers do not fall in line, they not only do not get what is legitimately due, but may also face false and fabricated charges.

TSR Subramanian, former Cabinet Secretary, writes,

> "I have frequently come across false and spurious cases mounted against innocent civil servants by vengeful superiors and politicians. It is easy to start a vigilance inquiry on flimsy and politically motivated grounds. Once the wheels are set in motion, nobody will take interest to close the inquiry. For a variety of reasons these false allegations are on the rise.
>
> The malaise has now spread to central investigating agencies, which hitherto had a spotless reputation for probity. The practice of mounting false cases by even hitherto uncorrupted central agencies on political grounds is very much on the increase. This has the potential to destroy the system."

Although the political environment has not been conducive to nurturing and promoting the civil service ethos, part of the blame for this malaise lies with the civil services as well. It is unfortunate that despite adequate constitutional safeguards against capricious action by the political executive, civil services in India have not been able to adhere to the values of honesty and political neutrality. For every officer who may be transferred for taking a principled stand, there may be half a dozen willing to compromise on principles, in their self-interest. The higher civil services have not been able to foster and maintain civil service ethos and camaraderie, a weakness that the political system exploited to demoralise and weaken them.

India is fast turning into a lawless society because of political, bureaucratic and judicial corruption, and a totally demoralised civil service. The country does not seem to be governed by the rule of law any more. In the public mind, the government is now perceived as a weak, corrupt and inefficient organisation. Criminals are making steady inroads into the political arena and if Parliament and State Legislatures do not shut their doors firmly to these elements, soon we may be governed by criminals. But our political class has shown little concern over this creeping onslaught on our parliamentary democracy. This may be seen by its readiness to reverse every decision of the Supreme Court and obstruct every effort of the civil society to bring in political reform. The price of allowing matters to drift may be too high for a country of India's size, ethnic and linguistic diversity, economic disparity, and hostile neighbours, and short history of national unity and democratic governance. The results of the 2013 election to the Delhi Assembly, where the nascent Aam Aadmi Party had spectacular results, might trigger churning in our political parties and force them to work for political reform.

Agenda for Future

If we have to restore rule of law and good governance, we need to reform both the political and civil service systems and clearly define their boundaries. New institutional arrangements need to be created and nurtured to remove the aberrations that have cropped up in our governance.

There are four major reasons for strained relations

between politicians and civil servants who believe in principles of political neutrality, honesty and objectivity.

1. The most important reason for tension is the conflict between a politician's interest in supporting his constituents and promoting his party's interests, at the cost of public interest, and a civil servant's concern with impartial and objective application of policy, law and rules.
2. There is no enforceable code of conduct for the political executive similar to the one prescribed for civil servants. Civil servants can at best put their views on record but cannot prevent wrong decisions being taken or implemented. The only recourse against misuse of political power is the loss of power in an election, which is too remote to be an effective deterrence.
3. At times, there is a wide gap between the education levels and intellectual attainments of civil servants and their political masters. Some civil servants, therefore, have a sense of superiority complex. Some politicians derive vicarious pleasure in insulting and deriding civil servants.
4. Civil society groups and the media have become quite active in recent years, and have made a significant contribution in espousing public anger against maladministration. But they have not been able to exert enough pressure to demand good conduct from elected representatives. Persons with criminal backgrounds can get elected and even become ministers.

The first and the most important step to restore civil service values and bring about a harmonious relationship between the Civil Service and political executives is to create institutional arrangements that will depoliticise the civil service and restore its autonomy, political neutrality and integrity. An environment needs to be created where these qualities are promoted and nurtured. In order to do so, it may be worth looking at the experience of other countries.

Institutional Arrangements in Other Countries

Among the economically developed countries, Japan and Singapore stand out as countries where relations between the political executive and the Civil Service are the most cordial and harmonious. After the Second World War, a number of prime ministers of Japan were former civil servants. Similarly, many seats in Diet (the Japanese Parliament) are held by former civil servants. The civil service has played a major role in rapid economic growth in both these countries and is held in high esteem.

There is a sharp contrast in the evolution of civil service systems after the Second World War in Japan and Singapore on the one hand, and India on the other. When occupation forces left Japan after the Second World War, Japan did not have a merit-based bureaucracy. Nor did it have an institutional mechanism to promote and nurture good civil service ethos. However, in the National Personnel Authority, it created a powerful and independent institution which has enabled Japan to have one of the best civil services in the world. The National Personnel Authority in Japan is an independent body that has remained politically neutral and is responsible for recruitment, promotion, retirement, training, remuneration, working hours, welfare, ethics and hearing of complaints from the employees. When Singapore got its freedom from colonial rule, it had one of the most corrupt civil services. It is a tribute to its political leadership that Singapore is now considered one of the least corrupt countries. In contrast, India, which had one of the best civil services in the world at the time of independence, now has one of the worst!

Creation of an Independent Civil Service Board

We should create a Civil Service Board on the lines of the National Personnel Authority of Japan, in order to create an enabling environment in which civil service ethos of political neutrality, honesty and efficiency can be promoted and nurtured. It is heartening to note that the Supreme Court has in a recent judgment recognised the need to create Civil Service Boards at the central and state level. This judgment has received a mixed reaction from the stakeholders. While some have welcomed it, as the first step in restoring the morale of the civil service, others have viewed it as an effort to remove political control over bureaucracy and an onslaught on the concept of democracy.

There can be no second opinion about the supremacy of the political executive in a democracy. A Civil Service Board is not meant to take away the powers of the political executive to supervise and control the civil service. It is essentially meant to insulate the civil service from arbitrary and capricious actions of the political executive. The 2013 suspension of a young IAS officer, Durga Shakti Nagpal, is a shining example of arbitrary and capricious action on the part of the political executive and the inability of the Chief Secretary to even give objective and honest advice to the Chief Minister against such action. Far worse was the boast of a leader of the sand mafia, that he was able to secure the suspension of an IAS officer in a jiffy. It is to control these kinds of actions that we need an independent and strong Civil Service Board.

A Civil Service Board should be politically independent and report to the Cabinet. This Board should be responsible for all service matters of officers of the level of Joint Secretaries and above, including empanelment, promotion, posting, transfers, and disciplinary action, including permission for investigation and prosecution by the CBI.

Members of the Board should be selected by a committee comprising the Prime Minister, the Chief Justice of India and the Leader of Opposition in the Lok Sabha. To maintain the supremacy of the political executive, the Board should make recommendations to the Appointments Committee of the Cabinet (ACC) for a final decision. If the ACC disagrees with the recommendations, it should record the reasons for such disagreement. The Board should include all such cases in its annual report to the Parliament.

The Board should hear and determine appeals in cases of concern about propriety and conscience raised by civil servants. It should also look into complaints of blackmail, intimidation and harassment, including false and malicious complaints by elected representatives. Where necessary, it ought to provide legal assistance to vindicate their position in a court of law, by filing libel suits. Civil Services Boards should also be constituted in States with similar functions for senior officers of the State Government.

Security of Tenure for Civil Servants under the Statute

A minimum tenure of two or three years should be mandated by law for all civil servants. Reasons for premature transfers should be recorded and communicated to the officer concerned, who must have a right to represent against such transfer.

Extension of Service and Post-Retirement Appointments under the State

The practice of extension of service or re-employment after superannuating as members of UPSC, CAT, Chairman and Members of regulatory authorities, etc., erodes the ability of senior officers to maintain neutrality and objectivity towards the end of their service. Some senior officers tow the lines of their political masters against their better judgment, in the hope that they may be able to secure a post-retirement assignment. It ought to be possible for the government to find suitable serving officers to man the positions offered to retired officers. It would be far better to increase the age of retirement to 65 years, instead of giving extensions and post-retirement assignments to a select few.

Speedy Action for Misconduct

It is often argued that transfer is the only effective tool available against erring officers because of the job security provided and long delays in completion of disciplinary proceedings. This argument is true to an extent. But transfer is not a solution to the problem of inefficiency or misconduct. By transferring inefficient or corrupt officers from one place to another, we do not solve the problem. We merely shift it. The proposed Civil Service Board should be mandated to weed out inefficient and corrupt officers and complete disciplinary proceedings in a time-bound manner.

CODE OF CONDUCT

Code of Conduct for Civil Service

The conduct of civil servants in India is guided by the Central Civil Services Conduct Rules and similar rules framed for All India Services and the members of State Civil Services. Conduct Rules in India are essentially a negative list of what civil servants should not do. In contrast, the Code of Conduct for the British Civil Service emphasises core values of the civil service. It would be worth looking at some of the provisions of the Code of Conduct adopted for the British Civil Service.

> "As a civil servant, you are appointed on merit on the basis of a fair and open competition and are expected to carry out your role with dedication and a commitment to the civil service and its core values: integrity, honesty, objectivity and impartiality. In this Code:
>
> - Integrity is putting the obligations of public service above your own personal interests;
> - Honesty is being truthful and open;
> - Objectivity is basing your advice and decisions on rigorous analysis of the evidence; and
> - Impartiality is acting solely according to the merits of the case and serving equally well governments of different political persuasions."

These core values support good governance and ensure the achievement of the highest possible standards in all that the civil service does. These in turn help the civil service gain and retain the respect of ministers, parliament, the public and its customers.

As far as relationship with a minister is concerned the Code stipulates:

"You must:

- Provide information and advice, including advice to ministers, on the basis of the evidence, and accurately present the options and facts;
- Take decisions on the merits of the case; and take due account of expert and professional advice;
- Not ignore inconvenient facts or relevant considerations when providing advice or making decisions; or
- Frustrate the implementation of policies once decisions are taken by declining to take, or abstaining from, action which flows from those decisions.
- Serve the government, whatever its political persuasion, to the best of your ability in a way which maintains political impartiality and is in line with the requirements of this Code, no matter what your own political beliefs are;
- Act in a way which deserves and retains the confidence of ministers, while at the same time ensuring that you will be able to establish the same relationship with those whom you may be required to serve in some future government; and
- Not act in a way that is determined by party political considerations, or use official resources for party political purposes."

"If you have a concern, you should start by talking to your line manager or someone else in your line management chain. If for any reason you would find this difficult, you should raise the matter with your department's nominated officers who have been appointed to advise staff on the Code.

If you have raised a matter in accordance with the relevant procedures, and do not receive what you consider to be a reasonable response, you may report the matter to the Civil Service Commissioners. The Commissioners will also consider taking a complaint directly."

These provisions reinforce the core values of the civil service and provide an institutional mechanism to officers at all levels to resist illegal orders issued by their superiors. It may be worth incorporating some of these ideas in the Civil Service Code in India.

Code of Conduct for Political Executive and People's Representatives

Members of Parliament and State Legislatures are expected to observe an exemplary standard of conduct both inside and outside the House in order to maintain the highest standards of parliamentary life and enhance the dignity of the House and its members. They also set the tone for disciplined conduct and respect for rule of law for the common citizenry.

In practice, however, the conduct of members is far from what is expected of them both inside and outside Parliament and Legislatures. Our parliamentary proceedings are one of the most unruly; fist-fights, hurling of missiles and chaotic behaviour are of daily occurrence. Outside Parliament too there is nothing much to write home about. Charges of corruption, horse-trading, extortion, blackmail and intimidation are often levelled against parliamentarians and other elected representatives. While the House has the right to punish members for misconduct, which includes admonition, reprimand, suspension, expulsion and even imprisonment, Indian Parliament and Legislatures have a dismal record of enforcing discipline and good conduct of their members.

In pursuance of the recommendations of the Santhanam Committee, the Central Government announced a comprehensive code of conduct for Central and State Ministers. In 1967 another Code of Conduct was drafted by the union home ministry for legislators. The code sought to bring together at one place the recognised principles and conventions which should regulate the relationship between Members of Parliament and State Legislatures on the one hand and civil servants on the other. The Code enjoined upon all civil servants to help members of legislature to the extent possible in the discharge of their functions under the Constitution. The Code simultaneously placed obligations on the legislators too. Legislators, it said, should ask for information only about public interest or national interest and should refrain from taking up individual cases concerning grant of permits and licenses, recruitment, promotion, transfer and disciplinary action. They should not seek information to further private interest or to give undue advantage to some individuals against others.

The Vohra Committee in its report submitted to the government of India in August 1995 clearly brought out the nexus between criminal gangs, police, bureaucracy and politicians. This report was discussed in Parliament and subsequently, following a meeting of all parties chaired by the then home minister Mr Chavan, it was decided to set up a Parliamentary Committee on Ethics as distinct from the Committee on Privileges.

An Ethics Committee was constituted by the Chairman of the Rajya Sabha in March 1997. After visiting the parliaments of UK, France, Finland and Italy, and after studying the codes of several countries, the Committee drafted a Framework of Code of Conduct for Members of the Rajya Sabha. However, except for parliamentary conventions, no Code of Conduct is as yet applicable to the political executive in India.

Codes of conduct for Members of Parliament have received more attention over the past few years in several countries, fuelled in part by the scandals tarnishing the public image of the institution and its representatives. The code serves as a guide to appropriate behaviour in daily work. A code can prescribe standards of behaviour in great detail, thereby reducing uncertainty for parliamentarians. In so doing, it provides the foundation for responsible action and ethical decision-making. It also provides a sound basis for disciplinary action in case of breach.

Codes can sensitise members of the public to the standards of behaviour they can expect from their representatives, they promotes public trust in the institution of Parliament and its members by publicly displaying the values and norms guiding legislators. Codes of Conduct are more specific than a Code of Ethics in terms of the actions prescribed and proscribed. They leave less to discretion; they are less aspirational and more prescriptive. Codes of conduct are usually more focused on the core functions of an organisation, rather than general ethical ideals that a decent person ought to abide by.

A number of countries including the US, the UK, Canada, Australia and New Zealand have adopted a Code of Conduct for Members of Parliament and Ministers. The basic principles enshrined in these codes are:

Selflessness: Holders of public office should take decisions solely in terms of public interest. They should not do so in order to gain financial or other material benefits for themselves, their family, or their friends.

Integrity: Holders of public office should not place themselves under financial or other obligation to outside individuals or organisations that might influence them in the performance of their official duties.

Objectivity: Holders of public office should make choices on merit in carrying out public business, including making public appointments, awarding contracts, or recommending individuals for rewards and benefits.

Accountability: Holders of public office are accountable for their decisions and actions to the public and must submit themselves to whatever scrutiny is appropriate to their office.

Openness: Holders of public office should be as open as possible about all the decisions and actions they take. They should give reasons for their decisions and restrict information only when the wider public interest clearly demands so.

Honesty: Holders of public office have a duty to declare private interests relating to public duties and to take steps to resolve conflicts in a way that protects the public interest.

Leadership: Holders of public office should promote and support these principles by leadership and example.

The British Parliament has adopted a detailed Code of Conduct for Members of the House of Commons. It has also created a fairly effective arrangement for enforcement of the code. We ought to create a similar code of conduct for elected representatives at different levels of governance.

Code of Conduct for Ministers

Some countries, notably the UK, have a detailed code of conduct for ministers. Apart from procedural guidelines, the code also prescribes norms of behaviour in regard to party interest, private interest, fund collection and a minister's relationship with civil servants.

It would be of interest to quote from the chapter on civil servant-minister relationship of the British Ministerial Code:

> "Ministers have a duty to give fair consideration and due weight to informed and impartial advice from civil servants, as well as to other considerations and advice, in reaching policy decisions; a duty to uphold the political impartiality of the civil service, and not to ask civil servants to act in any way which would conflict with the Civil Service Code; a duty to ensure that influence over appointments is not abused for partisan purposes; and a duty to observe the obligations of a good employer with regard to terms and conditions of those who serve them. Civil servants should not be asked to engage in activities likely to call in question their political impartiality, or to give rise to the criticism that people paid from public funds are being used for political purposes."

Ministers have been debarred from giving directions to civil servants that may conflict with the Civil Service Code. This is a salutary provision to ensure the neutrality and integrity of the civil service. It would be worth adopting a similar Code of Conduct for Ministers in India.

Enforcement of the Code of Conduct

If implemented properly, Codes of Conduct have the potential to considerably improve behavioural standards and increase adherence by civil servants and elected representatives to the values they can legitimately be expected to uphold. An improperly enforced code of conduct would, however, do little more than fuel the cynicism and mistrust of the citizens it sets out to resolve.

While a detailed Code of Conduct exists for civil servants in India, its implementation has been far from satisfactory. While the code bars civil servants from bringing extraneous influence to service matters, it is well known that a large number of officers at all levels including senior IAS and IPS officers peddle influence through political connections for plum posts. A large number of letters that come to ministers from MPs and MLAs are about service matters of employees in the government and its PSUs. No action is ever taken against the officers or politicians concerned. Political leaders frown upon resistance to such unwarranted pressures, irrespective of party affiliation.

The Code of Conduct for civil servants can be enforced more effectively and impartially if the responsibility for implementing it is transferred to an independent Civil Service Board.

There has been a long debate on how to enforce Codes of Conduct for ministers and other elected representatives, in countries where they have been implemented. Three options have been adopted in different countries.

1. Enact law and create an external implementing agency independent of Parliament and Legislature. This agency administers the Code, oversees the conduct of members, investigates into complaints, and reports to Parliament and Legislature. A few states of Canada have adopted this option.
2. Create a body within Parliament and Legislature, by a resolution, to oversee the conduct of members. Parliament may appoint a Commissioner to investigate complaints and report to a Committee of Parliament. The UK has adopted this approach.
3. Entrust the implementation of the Code of Conduct to the Ethics Committee of Parliament. The USA has adopted this option.

It is desirable that an independent Commissioner is appointed in India by enacting appropriate law to implement a Code of Conduct for Ministers, Members of Parliament and Legislatures, and other elected representatives. This would ensure that the code is enforced strictly. It would also enhance its credibility among citizens.

Towards a Harmonious Relationship

Cordial and harmonious relations should automatically follow if the political executive and civil servants clearly understand and respect the boundaries of their rights and responsibilities, and function within these boundaries. When Codes of Conduct are adopted and implemented effectively, as have been listed here, it can bring about greater accountability. It can result in required behavioural changes in the civil service and the political executive and create an environment of trust and mutual respect. This is essential for good governance.

Who is at the Helm?

No institutional arrangement can deliver results unless the people who man the institutions are persons of credibility, calibre and integrity. It would be worth our while to recall the concluding remarks of Dr Rajendra Prasad, when the Constituent Assembly adopted the Indian Constitution:

> "Whatever the Constitution may or may not provide, the welfare of the country will depend upon the way in which the country is administered. That will depend upon the men who administer it. If the people who are elected are capable and men of character, they would be able to make the best even of a defective Constitution. If they are lacking in these, the Constitution cannot help the country."

Epilogue

I do not recall the precise moment when I thought of writing this book. But it was a long time ago. After I retired, I started recollecting and recording various incidents that happened in the course of my service. I, however, did not know what to focus on. Then, the Second Administrative Reforms Commissions (ARC), headed by Mr Veerappa Moily, requested me to prepare a discussion paper on the 'Relationship Between the Political Executive and the Civil Service'. This paper never came up for discussion in the ARC deliberations. But it inspired me to write about my experiences in dealing with MLAs, MPs and Ministers. The CAG report on Coalgate came while I was in the midst of writing. The CAG was unfairly accused of overstepping his constitutional mandate and contributing to policy paralysis and slowdown of the economy. This prompted me to write a chapter in his defence. Then, the CBI registered an FIR against Mr Kumar Mangalam Birla and me for alleged conspiracy and corruption in coal block allocation. It, therefore, became imperative to bring the full facts into the public domain and call the bluff of the CBI. Hence, another chapter on Coalgate and the CBI.

Some individuals have come up for adverse comments

while narrating the incidents that happened in the course of my service. This is inevitable in a work of this nature. However, the purpose of this book is not to denigrate or criticise but to place in proper perspective, the problems and difficulties that civil servants face in the line of duty as mandated by the Constitution. I do not harbour ill will or contempt towards anyone. People may have had their own compulsions in acting or behaving as they did. At a personal level my relationships have remained cordial with many although I may have had differences in the course of my work.

Mr Rao and Mr Soren, both were courteous and warm. Mr Rao used to generally have meetings and briefings at his residence. He was hospitable and used to entertain lavishly. He often sent us prasadam, and homemade Andhra pickles and chutneys. He also organised a farewell luncheon for me when I retired, inviting all the Andhra cadre officers in Delhi and also presented gifts to my wife and me. Even Mr Chandra Shekhar Dubey, with whom I had a running feud, was decent enough to contribute ₹ 5 lakh from his Local Area Development Fund when I organised a camp to provide artificial limbs to physically challenged persons at Dhanbad. He also shared stage with me, at the inaugural function.

If this book can inspire the younger generation of civil servants to stand their ground in the face of political or other pressures and discharge their duties without fear or favour, its purpose would have been served.

ANNEXURES

Annexure 5-I

SECRET

P.C. PARAKH, I.A.S.
Collector & Dist. Magistrate

Kurnool
Dated: 06-04-1981

Dear Sir,

After discussing with you about the desirability of my continuing at Kurnool, I had met Hon'ble Minister of Law Sri E. Ayyapu Reddy at his residence to invite him to the inaugural function of Nandyal Co-operative Sugar Mills. The Hon'ble Minister enquired of me as to how could I straight away go to the Chief Minister and request him for the inauguration of sugar factory, meaning thereby that I should have made prior consultation with him, he being the Minister in-charge of the district. I explained to him that to my understanding, the Minister in-charge is to preside over the Zilla Parishad Advisory Committee meetings in the absence of an elected Zilla Parishad and generally review the development activities in the district. It is not necessary for the Collector to consult him on every matter relating to administration of the district. I had requested the Chief Minister to inaugurate the sugar mill in my capacity as Chairman of the Board of Directors of the sugar mill which is an autonomous institution and therefore, I did not feel it necessary to consult him before inviting the Chief Minister for the inauguration.

The Hon'ble Minister thereon stated that if I think that I must rule the district, where is the need for me to seek his cooperation. I told him that there was no question of my ruling the district and I am discharging my functions as the District Collector in the manner I consider most appropriate. The Minister there upon observed that I have not been discharging my duties properly and that there are charges of corruption against me. I requested him to be specific and let me know of any instance that has come to his notice. He mentioned that he had information that Sri C. Rami Reddy (the former BDO of Dhone, whom I had recommended for suspension and who has since been transferred to Srikakulam in view of his alleged complicity in disposal of NREP rice in the open market) had supplied cement for construction of my house at Hyderabad. The Hon'ble Minister perhaps did not know that most of the work of my house requiring cement had already been completed even before I took charge as the Collector of Kurnool district. I was astonished to hear this wild and baseless allegation from the Hon'ble Minister. After requesting him that if he had any information it would be appropriate for him to send a written complaint to the Chief Secretary or the Vigilance Commissioner, I took leave of the Minister.

During the course of the discussions, the Minister observed that he is not getting due consideration as Minister in-charge of the district and instead of the Collector, Superintendent of Police and Sub-Collector calling on him when he visits the district, perhaps it may be necessary for him to call on these officers. I explained to the Hon'ble Minister that according to the prescribed protocol the Collector and Superintendent of Police are required to call on the Minister during his first visit. It is not necessary for them to call on him on each subsequent visit, as it is neither prescribed in the protocol nor is it possible in view of pressing demands on the time of these officers. The minister perhaps feels that having been designated minister in-charge of the district; he is entitled to privileges over and above those prescribed under the normal protocol instructions. As there is no district officer in-charge of the subjects of the Hon'ble Law Minister, and therefore, no district level officer is accompanying him on his tours, the minister feels that he is not getting due importance in the district. However, the absence of a district officer cannot be made up by the Collector and the Collector cannot be expected to follow him on his tours every time he comes to the district. In spite of several other pressing items of work I had sent the Joint Collector to accompany the minister for tour of his constituency even though the Joint collector and I had already visited most of the villages earlier. However, this is not possible on every visit of the minister.

Nandyal Sugar Factory is a major industrial project in the district with an investment of ₹ 7 crore. In view of its importance,

I have always thought it appropriate that the Hon'ble Chief Minister should inaugurate this factory and this was the common consensus amongst the committee of persons-in-charge. The Hon'ble Minister of Law had expressed his desire to inaugurate the sugar mill to the Managing Director of the mill last month. I had requested the Managing Director to inform the minister that in view of the importance of the industry in the district, I feel it appropriate if the Chief Minister inaugurates the mill. I am at a loss to understand that after having made it clear that it would be appropriate if the Chief Minister inaugurates the sugar mill, why should the Hon'ble Minister for Law be keen to inaugurate the mill and why should he take objection to my inviting the Chief Minister.

I was aghast to hear the baseless and wild charges of corruption coming from a responsible minister of the State Government. If the Hon'ble Minister knew that Sri C. Rami Reddy, the former BDO of Dhone, had supplied cement for the construction of my house, the minister was obviously aware of the misconduct of Sri C. Rami Reddy and should not have stood in the way of his suspension. It would perhaps have been more appropriate for him to agree with my proposal for suspension of the BDO in view of his personal knowledge of the misconduct of the BDO in having supplied cement to me. He should have mentioned that in addition to the BDO, the Collector is equally corrupt and, therefore, action should be taken against him also. The entire record of construction of my house is available for scrutiny by anybody and I have been keeping the government informed of the various loans I had raised during the construction.

In a district so ridden with factions, to my understanding it is inappropriate for the District Collector to align himself with particular group and seek instructions from them, whether it is led by the minister or anyone else.

As the Hon'ble Law Minister, who is the minister in-charge of the district, has serious reservations about my capacity to function as the District Collector and has also reasons to believe that I am a corrupt officer, it would be unfair to him, to the district and to me, if I am continued as the District Collector, Kurnool any longer. I therefore, request that I may be shifted from this place at the earliest.

I had tried to see you personally after my interview with the minister both on the evening of the 4th and forenoon of the 5th but as you were away from residence, I could not meet and apprise you of the developments before I left Hyderabad for Kurnool.

With kind regards,

Yours Sincerely,
(P.C. PARAKH)

To
Sri S.R. Ramamurthy, I.A.S.
Chief Secretary to the Government
Andhra Pradesh, Hyderabad
Copy to Sri U.B. Raghavendra Rao, I.A.S.
Secretary to Chief Minister, Andhra Pradesh, Hyderabad

Annexure 6-I

P.C. PARAKH, I.A.S.

Hyderabad
Dt. 08-02-1983

Dear Sir,

I should like to draw your attention to certain basic issues that arise out of my transfer from the Hyderabad Municipal Corporation within four months of my taking charge. These issues relate to norms of bureaucratic conduct and principals of personnel management in the government.

I have no authentic information about the causes leading to my transfer and can make a reasonable surmise on the basis of what I hear from different quarters. I understand that the reduced tempo of road-widening works led the government to believe that I have not been effective enough at my new assignment. This, however, appears absurd as the decision to stop road-widening works was taken after a detailed discussion held in your chambers in the presence of the Finance Secretary and the Secretary, Municipal Administration. I was given to understand that the corporation cannot recklessly take up works without reference to its financial resources and commit the government to huge expenditure. Subsequently, the government issued a memorandum directing the corporation to stop all works not yet grounded and close the works already started at a safe stage.

The basic question that arises is whether individual officers of the government are entitled to trespass the limits of their authority and commit the government to several crores of expenditure to earn personal popularity? Is the government prepared to condone such financial impropriety on the part of all its officers or is such privilege is available to a select few? Should those who trespass their authority be termed dynamic and those who function within the framework of their assigned roles be called inefficient? If such dynamism is to be encouraged, half a dozen government officers would be enough to render the entire financial management of the government into a chaotic condition.

The fact that most of the roads widened recently have developed potholes within six months of their laying is a matter of common knowledge. In spite of the roads having been widened, the motorists still prefer to drive on the old carriageway. Anyone who has driven on these roads knows that these are no better than country tracks.

The results of investigation into the quality of these works should alarm any government. Can one believe that bitumen used in road-winding is as low as 28 per cent of quantity check-measured? Can one believe that RCC deck slabs should start crumbling within two years? Can one believe that slabs thickness is only 60 per cent of what is check-measured? But these are all facts. And these are the results from the Masab Tank to Secretariat road and Road No. 1 of Banjara Hills on which all the 'VIPs' drive. What the fate of other roads is can be anybody's guess.

Not one of these roads confirms to specified standards. The metal used is uniformly oversized, consolidation is grossly inadequate, crest thickness is up to 50 per cent of check-measured thickness, and no regard has been paid to integrate the camber of widened portion to that of the original road. These roads will need huge amounts for maintenance and would be a perpetual liability for the corporation.

No wonder the road-widening works were carried out at extraordinary speed. If the opportunities to make money are unlimited and quality of work is no consideration, no dynamism is required. There will be enough built-in driving force to speed up the work.

But is speed synonymous with dynamism? Should the quality of work be sacrificed for speed? Should the corporation squander its meagre resources to make contractors rich? Should the government encourage this in the name of dynamism? These are some of the mute questions that call for an answer.

In the absence of any other rational reason, should I presume that my transfer was engineered by those who run the risk of being exposed? I wish it was not the case but I am afraid it is so.

Road-widening is not municipal administration. Overflowing and choked drains, stinking garbage heaps, arbitrary and callous tax assessments, low labour productivity, pilferage of fuel and poor fleet maintenance are some of the more pressing and urgent problems of the corporation. These problems need detailed study, careful analysis, and methodical planning and execution.

Should the government then allow officers enough time to think and evolve solutions to these problems, or keep shuffling them every three months? Does the government assess the suitability of an officer before giving him a posting? How, and by whom, is the performance of civil servants to be assessed? Should transfers and postings be in public interest or at whims and fancy?

I do not consider myself an aggrieved party. I am therefore, not seeking any redressal from the government. However, the issues raised in this letter are of fundamental importance from the point of view of the morale of bureaucracy. The government may do well to give a serious thought to them.

With kind regards.

Yours sincerely,
(P.C. PARAKH)

Sri B.N. Raman, I.A.S.
Chief Secretary to Government
Government of Andhra Pradesh
HYDERABAD

Annexure 6-II

EXPRESS

lore, Madurai, Cochin, Bombay, Delhi, Ahmedabad & Chandigarh

MONG ALL DAILY NEWSPAPERS IN INDIA

CITY

: Friday, February 11, 1983 16 Pages 65 Paise

Another IAS officer revolts

Express News Service

HYDERABAD Feb 10

In the footsteps of his controversial predecessor, Mr A V S Reddy, senior IAS official P C Parakh, who was special officer, of the Hyderabad Municipal Corporation (MCH) until a week ago, has taken up cudgels against the State Government for his being transferred without sufficient justification.

Mr Parakh feels that his transfer ordered within four months of assuming charge as the MCH special officer raises "certain basic issues relating to norms of bureaucratic conduct and principles of personnel management" in the Government.

He opines that the matter needs careful consideration of the Government and intelligentsia and that an informed public opinion is necessary to help the Government evolve a sound policy.

Unlike Mr A V S Reddy in also an IAS officer who in October last year sparked off a heated public controversy by issuing a press statement against "political interference" in the functioning of the officials and the outdated conduct rules in force for IAS men Mr Parakh has confined himself to questioning the frequent transfers which assume importance from the point of view of "morale of bureaucracy".

He asks: Is it proper for the Government to keep shuffling the IAS officers every three months instead of allowing them enough time to think and evolve solutions to problems? Does the Government assess suitability of an officer before giving him a posting? How and by whom is the performance of a civil servant to be assessed? Should transfers and postings be in public interest or at whim and fancy?

Mr Parakh has been serving in Andhra Pradesh since 1969. The posts he held in the past include joint commissioner of commercial taxes (enforcement), collector of Kurnool district and director of civil supplies.

The MCH has been headed consecutively by as many as four IAS officers since last year —Mr Arjun Rao (10-1-1981 to 4-8-1982) Mr A V S Reddy (7-8-1982) to 7-10-1982) Mr P C Parakh (7-10-1982 to 3-2-1983) and Mr R P Singh from 3-2-1983.

HIS SURMISE

Mr Parakh has no authentic information on the causes that led to his transfer from the MCH, but on the basis of what he has heard from different quarters, he has surmised that the Government had attributed the reduced tempo of road widening works in the city to his alleged 'ineffectiveness'.

'This is absurd' according to Mr Parakh because in a meeting held in the chambers of the Chief Secretary, he was given to understand that the MCH cannot recklessly take up works without reference to financial resources and commit the Government to huge expenditure. Indeed, a few days after the meeting, the Government had issued a memo directing the MCH to stop all works as yet not grounded and close works already started at a safe stage.

Mr Parakh, obviously referring to his predecessor Mr Arjun Rao's remarks that it is ironic that one who was allegedly 'considered guilty of financial improprieties' had been eulogised as dynamic and that the one who stopped the works according to government directive have been condemned as 'inefficient'.

Mr Parakh has also drawn the Government's attention to big potholes that the widened roads have developed within six months and furnished technical data to show that the new thoroughfares do not conform to specified standards.

He has complained that even on the road connecting Masab Tank with the Secretariat bitumen used was as low as 28 per cent of the quantity estimated and check measured; slab thickness was only 60 per cent of that which was estimated and check measured; metal was uniformly oversized, consolidation grossly inadequate and no regard was paid to integrate the camber of widened portion with that of the original road.

Mr. Parakh says that all these widened roads would require huge amounts for maintenance and prove a perpetual liability to the MCH.

The extraordinary speed with which the road widening works were executed during the tenure of Mr. Arjun Rao suggests the obvious in a situation where "opportunity to make money is unlimited and quality of work is no consideration", Mr. Parakh says.

He has also pointed out to the State Government that "road widening is not municipal administration" and that the MCH has to primarily tackle difficulties posed by overflowing or choked drains, clearance of garbage heaps, arbitrary tax assessments and such other problems which call for detailed study, careful analysis, methodical planning and execution.

Mr. Parakh now awaiting posting orders after relinquishing charge as special officer of the MCH, believes that his transfer has been engineered by those that run the risk of being exposed in the substandard execution of road widening works.

Annexure 6-III

13 B, Janata Co-operative
Housing Society
Begumpet
Hyderabad
Dt. 11-03-1983

My Dear Bhai Saheb,

I hope this finds all of you well. We are all fine here. It was, indeed, a great pleasure to meet and spend some time with you during your last visit to Hyderabad.

I am writing this letter to seek your opinion on the possibility of civil servants invoking the Law of Torts against the government. Early last month I was transferred from the Municipal Corporation of Hyderabad after the new government took over the state administration. Although my transfer was not motivated by political considerations, the circumstances in which it happened raise certain basic issues of importance to the personnel policy of the government and morale of senior civil services in this country. I have set out these issues in the letter which I addressed to the Chief Secretary to the Government of Andhra Pradesh, a copy of which I am enclosing herewith for your reference.

Although, it was not for the first time that I had to face a transfer for offending vested interests, it was, however, for the first time that the transfer was accompanied by attendant humiliation of alleged inefficiency.

As frequent transfers of civil servants, motivated by a variety of pressures, and in complete disregard to either public interest or morale of the services, have become the order of the day, it is necessary that some unconventional methods to deal with this problems are evolved. Since the higher civil services have also been highly politicised particularly after 1975, and are rapidly getting divided into splinter groups based on parochial and caste considerations, service associations do not seem to be capable of dealing with the problem.

I think the Law of Torts can be successfully invoked by a civil servant who is humiliated by frequent transfers which are motivated by consideration other than public interest.

As the Law of Torts is a dynamic law not restricted by written code and is continuously changing in response to new conditions and needs, it should be possible for courts to give adequate relief where interest of justice would appear to demand it.

I will feel obliged, if you could spare some time out of your busy schedule to advise me if I can sue the state government for damages for causing mental anguish, and injury to my reputation by its action. If this case succeeds, it would be a landmark in the evolution of Law of Torts in this country and may perhaps help in preventing further demoralisation of higher civil services.

I am also enclosing a few paper cuttings which should give an indication of how the general public feels about these issues.

I would be happy if you could kindly convey your opinion at the earliest. Usha joins me in conveying our regards to Bhabhi and affectionate compliments to Abhishek, Anita and Abhilasha.

With kind regards,

Yours sincerely,
(P.C. PARAKH)

Dr. L.M. Singhvi
B8, South Extension, Part II
NEW DELHI 110049

Annexure 6-IV

DR. L. M. SINGHVI

PHONES : 661300 and 664831

B-8, SOUTH EXTENSION PART II
NEW DELHI-110049

Personal

13.3.1983

My Dear Kanwar Sahib,

I received your letter this morning. I am writing to you immediately so as to avoid any delay.

You have raised a legitimate public issue. Ordinarily, transfers are not considered justiciable except when they are mala fide or without jurisdiction. In your case, it might be said that the transfer also carried the stigma of inefficiency with it. Perhaps there is nothing to prove that the transfer was on that basis, but records may show this to be so. The concept of mala fides is considerably extended and the matter in law is equally actionable.

Tort is the weakest branch of our law; it is in a primitive and archaic state in our country. Your suit for damages would no doubt cover new ground but that is why it is not possible to give an accurate prognosis. All I can say is that it would be worth a try. It may end up by a Government clarification. It may put the Government on the defensive. It would compel public attention and arouse public concern.

(Contd.)

Frequent transfers are also public wrongs or public torts. The officers' Association should also take active interest in this matter and make it a kind of Public Interest Litigation.

The issue ought to be discussed and raised by the Institute of Public Administration also.

This brings you and dear Usha my affectionate remembrances — which Kamalaji, Abhishek, Amita and Abhilasha join me.

Sincerely,

L. M. Singhvi

Shriyut P. C. Parakh,
IAS.

Annexure 6-V

CONFIDENTIAL

GOVERNMENT OF ANDHRA PRADESH
GENERAL ADMINISTRATION (SCD) DEPARTMENT

Memo. No. 389/SCD/83-2 Dt. 23.3.1983

...

Sub: Public Servants—Sri P.C. Parakh, I.A.S.,—Contravention of certain provisions of All India Services (Conduct) Rules, 1968—Regarding.

Ref: From Sri P.C. Parakh, IAS., letter, Dt. 8.2.83.

- - -

According to rule 6 read with rule 7 (1) of the All India Services (Conduct) Rules, 1968 no member of the service shall, in any radio broadcast or in any document published anonymously, pseudonymously or in his own name or in the name or of any other person or in any communication to press or in any public utterance, make any statement of fact or opinion which has the effect of an adverse criticism of any current or recent policy or action of the Central Government or a State Government without obtaining permission of the government.

2. It is noticed that under different captions and dates in the daily newspapers, viz., Indian Express, dt. 11.2.83: Deccan Chronicle, dt. 11.2.83: Eenadu, dt. 14.2.83 and Andhra Prabha, dt. 11.2.83: the contents of his letter cited have been published without obtaining permission of the government. The act of Sri P.C. Parakh, IAS, in having released the matter to the press without permission of the government constituted violation of the rules mentioned in para (1) above. He is, therefore, requested to furnish his comments in the matter so as to reach the government within a fortnight from the date of receipt of this memorandum.

B.N. Raman
Chief Secretary to Government

To
Sri P.C. Parakh, I.A.S.
Secretary to Commissioner of Commercial Taxes
Hyderabad

Assistant Secretary to Government

Annexure 6-VI

P.C. Parakh, I.A.S.

Hyderabad
Dt. 13.9.1983

To
The Chief Secretary
Government of Andhra Pradesh
Secretariat
Hyderabad

Sir,

Ref: Government Memo No. 389/SCD/83.2/Dt. 23.3.1983.

Kindly refer to the government memo cited in which I have been requested to furnish my comments regarding publication in the newspapers of my letter dated 8.2.1983 addressed to the Chief Secretary.

Before I offer my comments on the release of my letter to the press, I should like to briefly narrate the state of affairs as existed when I took over the office of Special Officer, Municipal Corporation of Hyderabad.

The staggering callousness in spending public money to enrich contractors and unscrupulous officials came home to me within a couple of days of my joining Municipal Corporation of Hyderabad. It becomes relevant here to mention my report to the Secretary, Municipal Administration, regarding repairs to the road, through which the Moharram festival procession was to pass. This estimate was a typical example of unholy alliance between local politicians, contractors and corporation officials to defraud the Municipal Corporation. And it was not an isolated instance of mischief. The road-widening works were in conformity with the order of the day. I do not need to mention here again the results of investigations which were taken up with the assistance of the Chief Engineer, National Highways, and reported to the government.

As I went into details of the working of different wings of the corporation, I found manifestations of the same malaise everywhere. The assessment and collection of property tax is callous and arbitrary, the parameters for fixation of ratable values are undefined and discretion of tax officials unlimited; variation in tax liability of identical buildings is unbelievable; the working of conservancy section is primitive and inefficient; labour productivity is poor, disposal of garbage is unscientific and unhealthy; fleet utilisation is very low; there is large-scale pilferage of fuel; overloaded drainage system is choking for want of scientific maintenance; works are executed in wrong order of priority and without reference to technical feasibility and city planning is reduced to mere granting of relaxations from existing building rules.

Three months is too short a period to even identify the areas of deficiency in an organisation as big as the Municipal Corporation of Hyderabad, not to talk of taking remedial action. It took me hours of painstaking study to understand the working of various sections of the corporation and identify the areas of deficiency. In less than four months I planned for better execution of road work with the collaboration of Central Road Research Institute, made a comparative study of financial position of all major corporations in the country to strengthen the resource base of the corporation, planned for a more scientific tax system by computerising assessment and collection of property tax by taking the assistance of Tata Consultancy, took up works and methods study in consultation with the Administrative Staff College of India to improve labour productivity of conservancy workers and involved the National Building Organisation to adopt low cost technology for slum housing.

I have mentioned above my approach to problems so the government can understand the frustration that overtakes an officer who is deprived of an opportunity to implement the schemes he has painstakingly worked out.

There are occasions when political compulsions prompt premature transfer of officers. But in such cases the Chief Secretary and at times even Chief Ministers have generally shown the courtesy of taking the officer concerned into confidence, before passing orders. At the time of my transfer the government was new and no such compulsions existed. I was therefore led to believe that my transfer was engineered by people within the bureaucracy for obvious reasons.

While most of us have now accepted transfers motivated by

political considerations as a fact of life, service colleagues manoeuvring transfers and postings of their colleagues to serve their own personal agenda is a regrettable new phenomenon. Unfortunately, with the office of the Chief Secretary having been devalued, there are no institutional safeguards to prevent such activities.

The good tradition of giving a reasonable tenure to an officer so that he can understand the problems of an assignment, work out solutions and implement them has been given the go-by. While frequent transfers, motivated by ulterior considerations, do no personal harm to the officer concerned, they have had the effect of damaging the entire fabric of civil services in the country with the result that most civil servants have either become servile and pliable slaves of their political masters or confirmed cynics having lost faith in their own capability as well as that of the government they serve.

It is unfortunate that the Indian Administrative Service with its cosmopolitan character, which was considered the hope of India's future, should have degenerated into splinter groups led by parochial and self-centered individuals who have neither the courage of conviction nor values in life.

All the issues I raised in my letter under reference and those I have raised above are out of anguish and concern for the health of the civil services. The government may perhaps recall the letter I had written to the Chief Secretary when I was transferred from Kurnool, where I served as Collector. I had spoken of equally important issues in that letter, which is probably gathering dust in the cupboards of the secretariat. If the government chooses to remain insensitive to vital issues affecting efficient administration, which is its *raison d'être,* the only way out for a conscientious public servant is to pose these issues before the people at large. Before I released my letter to the press, I waited long enough for the government to react to the issues I had raised. A well-informed public opinion is perhaps the only way to make an inert government stir and hence the need for releasing my letter to the press.

If after an officer has put in more than a decade of service, the government does not have adequate assessment of his competence to hold a particular job, there is something seriously wrong with the government's method of evaluation. The fact that even my successor has been transferred within seven months of his taking charge should more than prove the deficiencies in the government's personnel policy. It looks as though the government is indulging in a chess game and public good is of no consequence.

The rule 7(i) of the All India Services (Conduct) Rules, 1968 prohibits only 'adverse criticism' of the government and not criticism *per se*. The word, 'adverse' according to the Chamber's Dictionary means, 'injurious' or 'harmful'. I do not consider my criticism as injurious or harmful to the government. My criticism on transfers, taken in the right spirit should make the government evolve a more rational personnel policy.

The facts I mentioned regarding quality of works executed by the Municipal Corporation or other irregularities are based on the records of the corporation and there is nothing secret or confidential about them. I would have been well within my right to disclose these facts to the press in discharge of my official duties. To my understanding, therefore, I have not contravened any provision of All India Service (Conduct) Rules.

If the government for any reason comes to the conclusion that my going to the press was breach of conduct rules, I may mention that no rules of conduct can be cited to prevent a citizen in a free society from airing his views on issues which affect his obligations to fellow citizens, his rights, self-respect and dignity and the integrity of the government. The conduct rules have to change along with the changing needs and values of society. In a democratic society, they cannot be regimental and shut the mouth of a person against the larger interest of the people.

In the above paragraphs, I have tried to make it clear why I took the extreme step of writing and releasing my letter to the press. If lack of objectivity, decency and courtesy on the part of the government could be the subject matter of judicial scrutiny, I would have gone to a court of law instead of the press. Unfortunately it is not so.

I am surprised at the priorities of the state, which is not at all perturbed about the massive fraud perpetrated on the taxpayers of the twin-cities in the name of road-widening, but is seriously worried about the "breach of conduct rules", in release of my letter to the press. The publication of my letter in the press has not in any way harmed public interest. On the other hand it has educated people and created a better awareness amongst the citizens regarding malfunctioning of the government. What I wrote months ago about road works on the basis of my investigation can be perceived by every commuter in the twin cities using the roads today. What can be the future of a State whose ruling elite is incapable of distinguishing between right and wrong, between the sinned against and the sinner?

The government's bias against me has been apparent in its subsequent decisions of insisting on my joining the Commercial Taxes Department, in directing me to apply for leave in respect of period which ought to have been regularised as compulsory wait, and in permitting one of my senior colleagues to sue me without even examining the issues involved. By the same token of justice would the government permit me to sue the Chief Minister for making an irrelevant and unwarranted statement in April 1983, while replying to the question of a press correspondent which had the effect of creating a wrong impression in public mind, as if I had uttered lies in my letter to the Chief Secretary?

I had not sent my reply to the government earlier, thinking that the government, having caused enough embarrassment to itself by its action, would not like to pursue matters so as to suffer further embarrassment. But I see that the government, like the *Bourbons of France,* has learnt nothing from its past mistakes. I am quite convinced of the righteousness of my cause and nothing can deter me from pursuing my chosen values in life.

Yours faithfully,
P.C. PARAKH

Annexure 9-I

22-9-1997

Dear Sri Bangur,

Mr. Seetharamaiah, Vice-President (Finance) of the A.P. Paper Mills Limited, visited me at my residence. While leaving my residence, he left behind a carry bag containing bundles of Rs. 100 currency notes. Since the carry bag had a picture of Lord Venkateshwara, I thought he had brought prasadam from Tirupati. Soon after he left my residence, my daughter found that the bag contained currency notes. I immediately called Mr. Seetharamaiah at his residence and asked him to come and pick up the money immediately.

He came back to my residence about 10 pm, and on enquiry, informed that this money was given by the party to whom letter of intent for conversion of FBC boilers was issued. He indicated that this is part amount of the kickbacks for the government directors; a similar amount was paid to the promoter directors.

I am greatly concerned and pained at the entire incident. It is a clear indication of malfunctioning in the company and practice of kickbacks being taken by the officers at various levels from suppliers.

In the circumstances of the case, I request you to kindly immediately withdraw the letter of intent issued for FBC conversion job, call for an emergency meeting of the Capital Goods Committee, and institute a thorough inquiry into the FBC conversion contract.

I would suggest that Mr. D. Subba Rao, nominee Director and Sri Kamalakar, nominee of ICICI, should form an inquiry committee to investigate the entire affair and suggest remedial measures.

I shall be grateful for your immediate response and action.

With regards,

Yours sincerely,
(P.C. Parakh)

Sri L.N. Bangur
Chairman
A.P. Paper Mills Limited
7, St. George Gate Road
Hastings, Calcutta 700002

Annexure 10-I

CONFIDENTIAL

GOVERNMENT OF ANDHRA PRADESH
PUBLIC ENTERPRISES DEPARTMENT

C.No. 45/PSP/PE/2001. Date: 19-5-2001.

Based on the course of discussions at the last few meetings of the Cabinet Sub Committee on P.E.Reforms, I feel that I do not enjoy full confidence and support from the group of Ministers who are involved in the process of privatisation of Nizam Sugars Ltd.

2. Privatization of SLPEs is a very difficult and sensitive program and can not be implemented by Head of Public Enterprises Dept., alone without total support and cooperation from all those who are involved in the process. I feel that I have not been able to effectively communicate and convince the group of Ministers that the approach being suggested by the Implementation Secretariat is the best approach in the circumstances.

3. In the absence of total understanding between the Implementation Secretariat Group of Ministers, and the Chief Executives of the Companies concerned, the privatisation programme may not proceed as desired and may have serious financial and political implications for the Government.

4. I would, therefore, suggest that Government may consider appointing another suitable officer to head Public Enterprises Department who enjoys confidence of the Cabinet Sub Committee and group of Ministers, and who will be able to steer the program successfully.

5. In order to enable the Government to take a decision, I propose to proceed on two months earned leave with effect from the 28th May, 2001.

Prl.Secretary,
P.E.Dept.,

Chief Secretary

Copy to: Sri S.V.Prasad, IAS, Prl.Secretary to Chief Minister with a request to fix an appointment with the Chief Minister so that I can explain my position to him.

Annexure 10-II

Extracts from the report of the House Committee of the Andhra Pradesh Legislature that enquired Into the Irregularities by the Private Management of Nizam Sugars Limited, 31st of August 2006.

Page 57

"The Committee expresses appreciation of the above comments of Mr. Parakh, which highlighted the potential loss to the government in case of acceptance of the GEL proposal. Extent of this loss is ₹ 308 crore."

Page 68

"34(a) The Committee has earlier referred to the views expressed by Sri PC Parakh, IAS, former Principal Secretary of Public Enterprises Department, who was also in charge of IS in early 2001. In our view, he showed commendable perception of the consequences and implications underlying the acceptance of the unsolicited proposal of GELCON. In this connection he presented his views on the unsolicited proposal to the CSC in the meeting held on 1-05-2001 with absolute clarity to impress upon the CSC how it is undesirable for the government to accept the GEL proposal."

Page 72

The CSC decided in 7 meetings for re-advertisement of the 4 units after rejection of GEL proposals. But every time, one minister or the other interfered and prevented the advertisement under pressure from GELCON. In this connection the ministers named below played a dubious role.

1. *************
2. *************
3. *************

Page 73

It is clear that the CSC was fully aware that in case of approval of the unsolicited proposal, the government would sustain loss of more than ₹ 305 crore as explained by Sri PC Parakh. Against this background the unsolicited proposal was approved on 22-09-2001 only to favour GEL out of the way and against rules.

Annexure 14-I

Secret

Ministry of Coal
O/o Secretary (Coal)
....

The following issues were discussed with the Hon'ble Prime Minister this afternoon.

1. Appointment of Shri Shashi Kumar as CMD, CIL
2. Permission to be accorded to CBI to register a case against Shri M.K. Thapar, CMD, SECL
3. E-auction of Coal
4. Cabinet Note for introduction of open bidding system for Allotment of Captive Coal Blocks

A brief note on the issues is enclosed.

Encl: as above

17.01.05

(P.C. Parakh)
Secretary (Coal)
17.1.05

4. **Cabinet Note for introduction of open bidding system for Allotment of Captive Coal Blocks**

after approval of PM as Minister-in-Charge on introduction of open bidding for allotment of Coal block, a Cabinet Note for Allotment of Coal Blocks for captive mining based on open bidding system was submitted to MOS(C&M)/Minister (Coal) on 23.12.04. The return of the file with the approval of Cabinet Note is awaited. In order to introduce the system at the earliest, it is necessary to bring necessary Legislative amendment in the Budget Session of the Parliament, after approval of the policy by the Cabinet.

Annexure 17-I

Confidential

OFFICE OF MINISTER OF STATE FOR COAL

Sub: Appointment of regular CMD of Coal India Ltd.

The file on the subject was placed before me and with my observations dated 25th January, 2005, the file was sent to Minister of Coal. Minister of Coal concurred with my views and referred the same to Secretary (Coal).

2. It is recalled that PESB recommended a panel of two officers for the post of CMD, CIL viz:

i) Shri Shashi Kumar
ii) Shri V.K. Singh

For the reasons elaborated in the said file the proposal for appointment of Shri Shashi Kumar was not found acceptable.

3. Shri V. K. Singh, No. II in the panel recommended by PESB was not considered/deliberated. It was expected that the file will be re-submitted to Minister of Coal for his consideration for appointment of the second candidate. Instead, it has been understood that Secretary referred the matter to DOPT for obtaining the clearance of ACC on the issue. It is strange that an incomplete proposal has been referred to the ACC.

4. Secretary (Coal) may explain this deviation from procedure and put up the proposal for appointment of regular CMD of CIL to Minister of Coal.

5. This has the confirmation of Minister of Coal.

18/02/05

No. 629/MOS(C&M)/05

428/Secy/S
18/2/05

Secretary (Coal)

19.02.05

With reference to above note of MOS (C&M), kind attention is invited to the following Rules of the Government of India (Transaction of Business) Rules, 1961:-

Rule:3- Disposal of Business by Ministers:-

Subject to the provisions of these Rules in regard to consultation with other departments and <u>submission of cases to the Prime Minister, the Cabinet and its Committees</u> and the President, all business allotted to a department under the Government of India (Allocation of Business) Rules, 1961, shall be disposed by, or under the general or special directions of, the Minister-in-charge.

Rule:6- Committees of the Cabinet:-

There shall be Standing Committees of the Cabinet as set our in the First Schedule to these Rules with the functions specified therein. The Prime Minister may from time to time amend the Schedule by adding to or reducing the numbers of such Committees or modifying the functions assigned to them.

Rule: 11- Responsibility of Departmental Secretaries

In each department, the Secretary (which term includes the Special Secretary or Additional or Joint Secretary in independent charge) shall be the administrative head thereof, and <u>shall be responsible for the proper transaction of business and the careful observance of these rules in that department</u>.

Item (i) and (iv) of the First Schedule: Cabinet Committee on Appointments

(i) To take decisions in respect of appointments specified in Annexure I to this Schedule;

(iv) to decide all cases of disagreement relating to appointments to board-level positions in public sector enterprises between the Department or Ministry concerned and the Public Enterprises Selection Board ;

Annexure to First Schedule in relation to the other Departments (which includes Coal Ministry)

Appointment whether salaried or not, of-

(i) Chairman and other members of the Board of Management (including the Managing Director and the Financial Adviser, if the Financial Adviser is a Member of the Board of Management) of any State-owned public corporation, company or enterprise, except where such appointment is made ex-officio by Government;

2. It may be seen from the above rules that a decision on acceptance or rejection of the recommendations of PESB on appointment of CMD/CIL has to be made by the Appointments Committee of the Cabinet and not by the Minister –in-charge of the Department.

3. In this connection, kind attention is also invited to the clarification issued by the Department of Personnel and Training vide D.O. No. 27(16)EO/86(ACC)- Part dated 13th October, 1987 about the role of Minister-in-charge of Department vis-à-vis Appointments Committee of the Cabinet. It has been clarified in the para 8 of the D.O. letter for the recommendation of the PESB in respect of appointments to posts of Public Sector Enterprises specified in the Annexure to the First Schedule to the Government of India (Transaction of Business) Rules, 1961, will have to be necessarily be referred to the Appointments Committee of the Cabinet by the Minister concerned after setting out his views there on.

4. Since Minister-in-charge did not agree with the recommendations of PESB, in respect of Shri Shashi Kumar, full facts of the case including all the notings of the MOS (C&M) and Minister (Coal) have been submitted for the consideration of Appointments Committee of the Cabinet.

5. It is submitted that the responsibility for ensuring proper Transaction of Business and careful observance of the Transaction of Business Rules lies with the Secretary of the Department and in fulfilment of that responsibility, full facts of the cases along with the views of the Ministers have been submitted for the consideration of Appointments Committee of the Cabinet.

6. In view of the fact stated above , there is no deviation from the procedure prescribed in the Transaction of Business Rules of the Government of India in submission of proposals for appointment of CMD, CIL and hence no explanation from the Secretary is warranted.

7. As regards consideration of the case of Shri V.K. Singh, entire information about Shri V.K. Singh the second name in the panel including his vigilance clearance had been submitted as a part of the notings of the Department. Had the Minister decided to recommend name of Shri V. K. Singh in preference to that of Shri Shashi Kumar, same could have been incorporated in the reference made to ACC. There was nothing more to be added in respect of Shri V.K. Singh which needed re-submission file to the Minister (Coal).

Submitted for favour of information.

23.2.05

(P.C. Parakh)
etary (Coal)
23.2.05

MOS(C&M)

Minister (Coal)

Annexure 18-I

BCCL

भारत कोकिंग कोल लिमिटेड

[illegible]

Bharat Coking Coal Limited

(A Subsidiary of Coal India Ltd.)

कोयला भवन कोयला नगर

Koyla Bhawan/Koyla Nagar

धनबाद-826 005

Ref. No. CMD:ES:F-19:04: 604

6th December, 2004

Strictly Confidential

The Secretary,
Ministry of Coal,
Government of India,
Shastri Bhawan,
New Delhi.

Sub : Impediments in functioning of BCCL imposed by Sri Chandra Sekhar Dubey, Hon'ble Member of Parliament, Dhanbad.

Dear Sir,

As highlighted through various communications in the past, all efforts to enhance coal production through use of hired HEMM in isolated patches made by BCCL is systematically resisted by Sri Chandra Sekhar Dubey, Hon'ble MP of Dhanbad. Copies of the relevant newspaper cuttings are enclosed at Annexure – I.

2. Use of hired HEMM for extraction of coal and OB from isolated patches is one of the key thrust areas identified and recommended for implementation in the Revival Plan of the Company with full support of all Trade Unions. Adequate safeguard has been built in on the lines of the advise received from Solicitor General of India in an earlier similar case pertaining to Singareni Collieries Company Limited to ensure that no violation of Contract Labour (Regulation and Abolition) Act is involved. It is needless to state that BCCL is saddled with old equipment in its existing mines and is, therefore, not in a position to re-deploy any equipment for extraction of coal from such isolated patches including the coal on fire below the Dhanbad-Patherdih Railway line, otherwise prone to illegal mining. Implementation of the proposals contained in the Revival Plan would have enhanced the production of BCCL by at least 2 m. tones – mostly coking coal – which would have enabled BCCL to mobilise around Rs. 200 crores annually. Contracts for this purpose have been awarded through a system of open tendering after due approval of the Board of Directors in all cases.

3. The Hon'ble MP, however, has been resisting the implementation of these contracts, not by any legal means but by sheer show of force and by threatening and intimidating the concerned contractors. The complaints of the contractors in this regard have been sent earlier, as may be seen from the Annexure-II.

4. However, the Hon'ble MP in his communication dated 27.9.2004 to the Hon'ble Prime Minister of India objected to the use of hired machines for contractual removal of overburden , coal cutting, transporting work etc. A detailed reply to the said letter was sent, vide my letter No. CMD:ES:F-2(A):04:550 dated 29/30th October, 2004 - copy placed at Annexure – III .

5. In another instance, bonafide effort made by the Management to identify the unauthorised occupants of houses in the Bhuli Township was negated by the Hon'ble MP when he decided to join hands with the agitators against a census being carried out for this purpose. The relevant newspaper cutting and the covering letter under which the same was sent to your kind self is enclosed at Annexure – IV.

Contd. .. 2.

: 2 :

6. In retrospect, it may be seen that the Hon'ble MP has systematically frustrated all positive efforts made by the Management to increase coal production and the steps taken for getting back large number of Company houses occupied by persons in an unauthorized manner. Besides, the Hon'ble MP, within a few days of his being elected to the Parliament, held a press conference at Dhanbad in which he accused the CMD of BCCL being a " **MAFIA DON** ". This was communicated, vide my letter No. CMD:ES:F-2(A):04:330 dated 14.6.2004 along with the relevant press cutting (copy enclosed as Annexure – V). Subsequently the Hon'ble MP, on a number of occasions, have accused the undersigned publicly of being " **AGENT OF RSS** ", " **AGENT OF BJP** " etc.

7. I have not been able to comprehend the reasons for such behaviour on the part of the Hon'ble MP except for the fact that immediately on being elected he had asked for a D type quarter in the BCCL Township which I had to politely decline. In one of the closed door meetings, when Director (Technical) Planning & Projects and Director (Personnel), BCCL were accompanying me, the Hon'ble MP stated that he will act personally against me as I have declined him the house which, in his opinion, is due to him by virtue of being the MP of the District. Incidentally the earlier MP, Mrs. Rita Varma, has been occupying a house in BCCL since long time which was occupied by her following the murder of her husband – late Randhir Varma, the then Superintendent of Police, Dhanbad. She has since been issued a notice to vacate the accommodation at the earliest.

8. The stand adopted by the Hon'ble MP against allowing use of hired HEMM in BCCLfor producing coal and OB from isolated patches and/or carrying out census of its quarters to evict the unauthorized occupants will have the effect of dampening the efforts made by the Company for its Revival. Also without extra production from hired HEMM the Company will not be in a position to meet even a part of the additional liability on account of NCWA-VII.

9. Under the circumstances the matter may have to be taken up at the highest possible level for appropriate action.

Yours faithfully,

Encl : As above

(Partha S Bhattacharyya)
Chairman/Mg. Director

Annexure 18-II

CHANDRA SHEKHAR DUBEY
MEMBER OF PARLIAMENT
(LOK SABHA)

Member: Parliamentary Consultative Committee On Coal & Mines.

Room No.24
Hotel Janpth
New Delhi
Ph. 23349490

DATE -> 08-11-04

Respected Sir,

I am taking an opportunity to highlight a facts which needs special intention and personal intervention for the official position misused by the Coal Secy., Govt.of India. If such activities continues or repeated in future then there will a heavy loss to exchequer for misuse of huge foreign exchange for his vested interest.

Since Shri P.C. Parekh a Coal Secretary have been sanctioned an official tour to attend Mine Expo-2004 for two different countries but surprisingly he had extended his tour for four different countries including Switzerland for his personal transactions. If the senior official from the Govt. of India violates/misuses his official position and the Govt. guidelines, Rules & Regulations then may not expect from the others to follow the govt. directives.

As your goodself is aware that Coal Industry is an important Deptt. and back bone of our country for smooth running of the same the country needs a efficient and honest official rather than ignoring the manipulation or misuse of powers by the present Secy. of Coal. I understand that there is a heavy manipulation on the following which needs a proper investigations:

1. Shri P.C. Parekh was sanctioned a official tour for two different countries to attend MINE EXPO-2004 but he has extended his tour and visited four more different countries (including Switzerland for up dating his transactions) which has caused heavy loss to the ex-chequre by utilising huge Foreign Exchange.
2. He has also exercised his full powers and manipulated for nominating two Govt. Directors in CMPDI Board though the Govt. sanction was only for one Director.
3. The final approval of ACC for two nominee of Govt. in Coal India Board has been reduced to one by Shri Parekh.
4. He was also liaisoning for sell of the profit making Coal India Limited and hold personal meetings with the seeking bidders for number of times.

I shall be grateful if your goodself may immediate enquiry as stated above to curb the malpractices followed by Shri P.C. Parekh from any of the independent authority preferably either by C.V.C. or by Parliament Committee so that the truth be placed on the record.

With kind regards,

Yours sincerely,

8.11.04

(CHANDRA SHEKHAR DUBEY)

Dr. Manmohan Singh,
Hon'ble Prime Minister of India,
New Delhi.

Ack being put up separately

Annexure 18-III

P.C. PARAKH
SECRETARY

भारत सरकार
कोयला और खान मंत्रालय
कोयला विभाग
शास्त्री भवन, नई दिल्ली-110001
Government of India
Ministry of Coal & Mines
Department of Coal
Shastri Bhawan, New Delhi-110001

Telephone : 23384884
Fax : 23381678

D.O. No. Secy(C)/11019/04 Dated: 6.12.04

Dear Shri Chaturvedi

Please find enclosed a copy each of the letter addressed by Shri C.S. Dubey, Hon'ble Member of Parliament (Lok Sabha) from Dhanbad to the Minister of State for Coal & Mines making serious allegations against me and the office note submitted to the Minister of State for Coal and Mines in respect of these allegations explaining actual facts.

2. I am constrained to point out that the allegations made by Mr. Dubey are totally baseless and libellous in nature. He has alleged that I had visited "Switzerland for updating my personal transactions" implying thereby that either I have some bank account in a Swiss Bank or I had indulged in some other illegal personal transactions. After taking over as Secretary, Department of Coal I did not visit Switzerland at any time. It is,therefore, not known on what basis Mr. Dubey has made these allegations. Since an Hon'ble Member of Parliament has made serious allegations against a Secretary to the Government of India, the matter needs to be taken up in all its seriousness and should be investigated at the earliest. In case the allegations are found to be false and baseless Mr. Dubey should be made to face all such legal consequences (criminal and civil) that should follow under the Indian Law for making false allegations.

- 2 -

3. It would be of some interest to give a small background of the reasons for Mr. Dubey's ire. Soon after he got elected as a Member of Parliament, Mr. Dubey requested the CMD Bharat Coking Coal (BCCL) Shri P.S. Bhattacharya for allotment of one of the Company's houses to him at Dhanbad. CMD,BCCL sought my informal advice on this and I advised him against it as it will frustrate CMD's efforts for vacation of Company's houses which are in the illegal possession of outsiders. Years of mis-management, indifference, influence of mafia and complicity of officers of BCCL has led to hundreds of houses of the Company being occupied by outsiders. Mr. Dubey has been actively supporting the illegal occupants and frustrating the efforts of CMD,BCCL to get these houses vacated by illegal occupants. Keeping in mind the ground realities, allotment of a house to Mr. Dubey which he is not entitled to under Rules, would have strengthened the case of illegal occupants .

4. Incensed by the decision of CMD, BCCL not to allot the house, Mr. Dubey started a smear campaign against Shri Bhattacharya. Copies of some of the press cuttings of local newspapers, wherein Mr. Dubey has made serious allegations against Shri Bhattacharya are enclosed for your perusal. The utterances of Shri Dubey against Shri Bhattacharya are provocative and libellous.

5. At a recent Consultative Committee meeting of the Ministry of Coal and Mines held on 23.11.04 Mr. Dubey's utterances against me, to say the least were offensive and insulting. This was on account of my pursuing outsourcing of coal in BCCL which is indispensable if BCCL has to be brought out of the red.

- 3 -

6. Baseless allegations levelled by Mr. Dubey do not enhance the dignity of either the office of the Member of Parliament or that of the Secretary to the Government of India.

7. The Prime Minister in his recent address to the Secretaries to the Government of India, had emphasised the need for transparency, objectivity and morality in Public Administration and management of Public Sector Undertakings. If senior officers of the Government and Executives of the Public Sector Undertakings are blackmailed, insulted, intimidated and maligned, by the elected representatives of people it will have deleterious impact on the morale of the Civil Servants and the Executives of the Public Sector Undertakings.

8. It is requested that the matter may be placed for consideration of Prime Minister and Speaker of Lok Sabha for such action as they deem fit.

With regards

Yours sincerely,

(P.C.PARAKH)

Shri B.K.Chaturvedi,
Cabinet Secretary,
Government of India,
New Delhi.

Annexure 18-IV

P.C. PARAKH
SECRETARY

भारत सरकार
कोयला मंत्रालय
शास्त्री भवन, नई दिल्ली–110001
Government of India
Ministry of Coal
Shastn Bhawan, New Delhi-110001

Telephone : 23384884
Fax : 23381678

CONFIDENTIAL

No. 7192/Secy(Coal) 21st June, 2005

Dear Shri Chaturvedi

Please find enclosed a copy of letter addressed by Shri V.K. Singh, Chairman-cum-Managing Director, Northern Coalfields Ltd., to Chairman, Coal India Ltd. Shri Singh in his letter has referred to certain unreasonable demands made to him by Shri Narenda Kumar Kushwaha, Hon'ble Member of Parliament, Badhohi Mirzapur Constituency of Uttar Pradesh.

2. Non-compliance of these demands seems to have prompted the Hon'ble Member of Parliament to make complaint against Shri Singh. This is not a healthy state of affairs and may leads to demoralisation of senior executives of PSUs.

3. This is for favour of your information and necessary action as you deem fit.

With regards

Yours sincerely,

(P.C. Parakh)

Encl: as above

Shri B.K. Chaturvedi,
Cabinet Secretary,
Cabinet Sectt.,
Rashtrapati Bhawan,
New Delhi

Annexure 18-V

9708/Secy (C) 11/7

P. SHANKAR

भारत सरकार
केन्द्रीय सतर्कता आयुक्त

D.O. No. CVC/2005/87/1349

Government of India
Central Vigilance Commissioner

Central Vigilance Commission
Satarkta Bhawan,
GPO Complex, Block-A, INA, New Delhi-110023
Tel. 4651020 (O), 3384815 (R)
Fax 91-11-4651009

July 8, 2005

Dear Shri Parakh,

The Commission has perused your letter and the communication from CMD, NCL. The Commission has more than once noted that complaints even from such responsible persons as Members of Parliament often knowingly or otherwise become instruments of pressure and harassment of honest officials both in Government and in the public sector. Complaints received in the Commission are always carefully examined with total objectivity irrespective of the stature of the complainant. This cannot always be said when such complaints are processed in the administrative Ministries / Departments. In the Commission's view the solution lies in making the Central Vigilance Commission the focal point to deal with all complaints against officers of Government and PSUs who come within the purview of the CVC as per the CVC Act, 2003. No independent action should be initiated by any department or Ministry without the complaint having been perused and examined for advice by the Commission. This would create the necessary buffer between honest officials and vested interests and pressure groups.

2. While the Commission has been pursuing this seriously at various levels of Government, Secretaries to Government in important Ministries like you need to bring this up during discussions in the Committee of Secretaries and see that an appropriate decision is taken. The point really is that Ministries / Departments should not exercise independent powers of examination of complaints and initiation of action thereon without reference to the Commission. I hope you will be able to do this in the interest of efficient functioning of PSUs under your control.

With regards,

Yours sincerely,

(P. Shankar)

JS(C)

Shri P.C. Parakh
Secretary
Ministry of Coal
Shastri Bhawan
New Delhi-110 011

Annexure 18-VI

CONF IDENTIAL

भारत सरकार
कोयला मंत्रालय
शास्त्री भवन, नई दिल्ली–110001
Government of India
Ministry of Coal
Shastri Bhawan, New Delhi-110001

P.C. PARAKH
SECRETARY

Telephone : 23384884
Fax : 23381678

D.O.No.Secy(Coal)/8.8.05 Dated: 8.8.05

Dear Shri Chaturvedi

Kindly refer to my D.O. letter dated 21st June,2005 regarding motivated complaints against senior executives of Coal companies by the Members of Parliament. I had also brought this matter to the notice of the Central Vigilance Commissioner, for appropriate action.

2. Central Vigilance Commissioner vide his D.O.No.CVC/2005/87/1349 dated 8th July,2005 has advised that the issue may be discussed at a meeting of Committee of Secretaries. CVC has suggested that on complaints received against senior executives of PSUs no action should be taken by the Department/Ministry without the complaint having been first examined for advice by the Commission.

3. Suggestion made by CVC may be only a partial solution to the problem as it may not prevent Members of Parliament from making motivated and false allegations against senior officers of Government or Public Sector Undertakings. There is a need for the government to create appropriate institutional arrangement to ensure that Members of Parliament are not able to misuse their privileged position to blackmail or intimidate senior officers of the Government and senior executives of public sector undertakings.

4. You may like to advise the Department of Personnel to prepare a suitable paper for discussion at COS.

With regards

Yours sincerely,

/

(P.C.PARAKH)

Shri B.K.Chaturvedi,
Cabinet Secretary,
Cabinet secretarit
New Delhi.

Copy to Shri P.Shankar,CVC, New Delhi.

(P.C.PARAKH)

Annexure 18-VII

Anti-Corruption
(Secret)

प्रधान मंत्री कार्यालय
नई दिल्ली-110 011
PRIME MINISTER'S OFFICE
NEW DELHI - 110 011

V. VIDYAVATHI
DIRECTOR
Tel: 2301 8485

D.O. No. 600(AC)/31/C/28/(417)/05-ES.II 2nd August, 2005

Dear Sir,

Please find enclosed herewith a complaint received in PMO from Shri Furkan Ansari and Shri C.S. Dubey, Members of Parliament (Lok Sabha) against Shri R.P. Ritolia, CMD, Eastern Coal Field Ltd. alleging corrupt practices. The discreet inquiry into the allegations is summarized as under: -

(i) Shri R.P. Ritolia, CMD, CCL, has been holding additional charge of CMD, ECL since February, 2005, when the post fell vacant due to the retirement of the then CMD, ECL, Shri Abdul Kalam. Earlier, Shri Ritolia worked as Director(Project and Planning) at ECL Hqrs. and had earned a good reputation there. Enquires in the coal sector reveal that Shri Ritolia has the reputation of being a sincere and dedicated person who is liked by his colleagues.

(ii) Shri Furkan Ansari, MP had tried to get about 100 Muslims of Jamtara area employed in S. P. Mines, Chitra, Deoghar district. However, Shri Ritolia did not oblige.

(iii) No work regarding costing of OBR (overburdens) has been undertaken in the Mugma area of ECL and the grading of coal as A, B, C or D is done by the ECL's laboratory. Any alleged malpractices could not be confirmed.

(iv) As regards the allegation of rampant theft of coal taking place in the name of filling up the closed open cast project (OCP) in

-2-

Secret

प्रधान मंत्री कार्यालय
नई दिल्ली-110 011
PRIME MINISTER'S OFFICE
NEW DELHI - 110 011

the Mugma area, enquiries revealed that there are 12 collieries functioning in the area out of which 9 are underground and 3 are OCP. During 2000, 2 underground mines, Kapsara and Nirsa collieries were closed due to safety reasons, however, no OCP has been closed in the area. As the 3 OCPs are currently producing coal, the prospect of filling these OCPs does not arise. On the contrary, the CGM, Mugma area office has sent a proposal to ECL Hqrs. to open 4 new OCPs, by converting 2 of the closed underground mines (Nirsa and Kapsara) and 2 other loss making underground mines, Harijana and Sajna, into OCPs.

(v) In so far as the allegation of payments being made to contractors in filling up OCPs in Bajna collieries, it is learnt that it is actually an underground colliery project. However, the existence of coal near the soil surface has led to extensive illegal mining from the surface. In order to curb this, the ECL has spent nearly Rs. 4.85 lakh towards payment of contractors for filling up of the exposed area. Further, in order to stop illegal mining altogether, the ECL has drawn up a proposal for converting the loss making Bajna colliery into an open cast project. A proposal to this effect has been sent to CIL for approval.

(vi) As regard the SP mines in Chitra Colliery, it is learnt that inFebruary 2005, Shri Ritolia transferred the GM and the Agent, who are responsible for the day to day running of the mines and brought in Shri N.K. Singh, GM and Shri B.K. Singh, Agent, who are considered to be CMD's men. In the recent past, some excess payments are reported to have been made in

-3- **Secret**

प्रधान मंत्री कार्यालय
नई दिल्ली-110 011
PRIME MINISTER'S OFFICE
NEW DELHI - 110 011

respect of some civil work. However, the involvement of the CMD could not be substantiated.

2. I am desired to request that an appropriate reply may be sent to the Hon'ble Members of Parliament from Minister of State for Coal & Mines, and a copy may please be sent to this office.

With regards,

Yours sincerely,

(V. Vidyavathi)

<u>Encls : As above</u>

Shri P.C. Parekh,
Secretary,
Department of Coal,
Shastri Bhawan,
NEW DELHI.

Annexure 18-VIII

COAL INDIA LIMITED
Chairman's Secretariat
10 Netaji Subhas Road
Kolkata – 700 001

PHONE : 033 –22435063/22436679
FAX : 033 - 22483373
E-MAIL : chairmancil@vsnl.net

CIL:CH:CONF:584 17788/? 16/11 09th November, 2005

CONFIDENTIAL

The Secretary to Govt. of India
Ministry of Coal
Shastri Bhawan
New Delhi

This is regarding transfer and posting of one Shri P.K. Saha, SE(Excvn.). He has been transferred from BCCL to MCL at the instance of Hon'ble Shri Anant Kumar MP and Chairman, Standing Committee of Parliament for Coal & Steel. Shri Saha has already joined at MCL, HQ. In this connection, letter No. CMD, MCL dated 9th November, 2005 of CMD, MCL along with its enclosures (copy enclosed) may kindly be perused which indicate his organizational behaviour for his own benefit since beginning.

This morning (09.11.2005) Hon'ble Shri Anant Kumar, Chairman, Standing Committee of Parliament for Coal & Steel telephoned me and enquired about the case of Shri P.K. Saha, Supdt. Engr.(Excvn.). From what I could recall, I told him that Shri Saha had already been transferred to MCL. Hon'ble Shri Anant Kumar indicated to me that Shri Saha had to be posted at Kolkata Desk Office of MCL and instead of that he has been posted at Sambalpur, H.Q. of MCL by CMD, MCL. And on being approached for placement at Kolkata Desk Office of MCL, the CMD, MCL, Shri A. Sharma had talked nastily to Shri Saha and threatened that he would not yield to political pressure and Shri Saha would not be transferred to Kolkata Desk Office of MCL. In case he i.e. CMD, MCL was further pressurized, the consequences would be bad for Shri Saha. Political leaders need to understand that such pressures will not work.

Continuing further in the matter, Hon'ble Shri Anant Kumar told me that corrupted officials of CIL and MCL were doing all kinds of nonsensical things and not responding to the legitimate grievances of their officers. Such behaviour from CMD, CIL and CMD,MCL would not be tolerated by him (Hon'ble Shri Anant Kumar) and he (i.e. Hon'ble Shri Anant Kumar) and his party i.e. BJP would see to it that CMD, CIL and CMD, MCL realize their mistake and understand the value of the political leadership. He told that I would regret the day when Shri Saha's request was not acceded to and in the remaining ten months he would teach me a lesson and I would repent for my action. While maintaining my calm I requested him that he should come out of his agitated state of mind, so that I could understand and appreciate the problem to arrive at a logical conclusion but he did not agree to listen to me. He agreed that he was agitated and indicated that the reasons of his agitation lay in the irresponsible behaviour of CMD, CIL and CMD, MCL. I once again tried to assure him that the matter would be looked into and in case any action was required to be taken the same would be taken. But he said "enough is enough" and now I have to pay for my alleged misdemeanor. The conversation took place telephonically while I was busy in holding CMDs meeting. I, thereafter requested Shri A. Sharma, CMD, MCL to clarify the matter. Shri Sharma told that Shri Saha had approached him for his transfer to MCL Desk Office, Kolkata and in view of his request Shri Sharma had agreed to such placement for a period of 5 months upto March, 2006. But this was not acceptable to Shri Saha who wanted it for a period of at least 2 years.

In view of the above it may kindly be noted that Shri P.K. Saha, S.E.(Excvn.) is in the habit of putting pressure through different persons giving false statements regarding his family, which is obvious from the enquiries and remarks of Shri APVN Sharma, CVO, MOC and Shri RAP Singh, the then Director(Personnel), CIL. A brief case history of Shri P.K. Saha, SE(Excvn.) is enclosed herewith.

This is for your kind information.

Yours faithfully,

(Shashi Kumar)
Chairman

Encl: as above.

Annexure 18-IX

CONFIDENTIAL

No.177788/Secy©/2005
OFFICE OF SECRETARY(COAL)
SHASTRI BHAVAN,NEW DELHI.

Placed below is a letter received from Chairman,CIL along with enclosures about telephonic conversation between him and Shri Ananth Kumar,Hon'ble Member of Parliament and Chairman of the Standing Committee of Parliament on Coal and Steel.

2. Shri Ananth Kumar has threatened him for not complying with his request to transfer Shri P.K.Saha an Excavation Engineer in MCL to Kolkata Shri Saha is an Excavation Engineer and his services should be normally utilised at mine site. In stead of working in operational areas, Shri Saha has spent long years at Kolkata either by misusing the legal process by getting court orders or by bringing political pressure on the management of CIL.

3. The action of CMD,MCL in having posted Shri Saha at Company's headquarters at Sambhalpur after he has worked for several years in Kolkata cannot be found fault with. There is hardly any work for an Excavation Engineer at Kolkata office and there is no justification for retaining him at Kolkata as desired by Shri Ananth Kumar.

4. Intimidating and threatening language used by Shri Ananth Kumar against Chairman,CIL is not expected from a person of his standing who has been a member of the Union Council of Ministers and is currently Chairman of the Standing Committee of the Ministries of Coal and Steel.

5. Government's efforts at providing good governance cannot succeed unless political leadership creates an environment in which senior civil servants and executives of public sector units can act professionally, independently and impartially in the best interests of their respective organizations. If the position of chief executives of public sector undertakings is undermined by senior political leaders of the country, it can only encourage indiscipline and harm the interests of PSUs.

6. Submitted for favour of information and such action as PM & M(Coal) considers appropriate and necessary.

(P.C.PARAKH)
Secretary(Coal)
30.11.05

MOS(C&M)

Annexure 18-X

P.C. PARAKH
SECRETARY

भारत सरकार
कोयला मंत्रालय
शास्त्री भवन, नई दिल्ली–110001
Government of India
Ministry of Coal
Shastri Bhawan, New Delhi-110001

Telephone : 23384884
Fax : 23381678

D.O.No.Secy(Coal)/8.8.05 Dated: 8.8.05

Kindly refer to my D.O.letter No.Secy(C)/12019/04 dated 6.12.04 wherein I had requested you to bring to the notice of the Speaker of the Lok Sabha certain facts regarding conduct of Members of Parliament vis-à-vis civil servants that can have serious negative effect on the morale of civil services. I am not aware if the Hon'ble Speaker took any action on the concern expressed by me.

Conduct of Shri Dharmendra Pradhan, Hon'ble Member of Parliament from Orissa at the Consultative Committee meeting of the Ministry of Coal held on Friday the 5th of August,2005 leaves me in little doubt that we have descended to such low levels of working in our Parliamentary democracy that it is becoming increasingly difficult for the civil servants to function with self respect, dignity and professional integrity.

I feel it impossible to function in such a vicious environment and would like to be immediately relieved of my responsibilities as Secretary (Coal). This letter may be treated as my request for voluntary retirement. Pending approval of my request I am proceeding on earned leave with effect from the 9th of August 2005.

Yours sincerely,

(P.C.PARAKH)

Shri B.K.Chaturvedi,
Cabinet Secretary,
Cabinet Secretariat,
New Delhi.

Copy to (1) MOS(C&M), New Delhi
(2) Shri T.K.A.Nair,Principal Secretary to PM,

(P.C.PARAKH)

Annexure 18-XI

P.C. PARAKH
SECRETARY

भारत सरकार
कोयला मंत्रालय
शास्त्री भवन, नई दिल्ली–110001
Government of India
Ministry of Coal
Shastri Bhawan, New Delhi-110001

Telephone : 23384884
Fax : 23381678

D.O.No.Secy(Coal)/22.8.05 Dated: 22.8.05

Dear Shri Chaturvedi,

Kindly refer to my D.O. letter No.Secy(Coal)/8.8.05 dated 8.8.05 wherein I had applied for voluntary retirement and requested for sanction of earned leave with effect from the 9th of August. I had to take this step in view of insulting and derogatory language used by Shri Dharmendra Pradhan, Member of Parliament at the Consultative Committee meeting.

In order to express my anguish and concern that such conduct on the part of Member of Parliament can leave on the morale of civil service and senior executives of Public Sector Corporations, I had sought for and had a meeting with the Hon'ble Prime Minister on the 17th August. The Prime Minister expressed his regret at what transpired at the Consultative Committee meeting and advised me not to press for the premature retirement.

While confirming his full confidence in me the Prime Minister also offered to address officers of Coal Ministry and Coal India Limited to reassure them of his confidence and support. This gesture on the part of the Prime Minister will definitely help restore morale of my officers, which was completely shattered due to unfortunate incident of the 5th August.

I am grateful to the Prime Minister for the confidence and support. In the light of facts stated above, I am withdrawing my request for premature retirement.

I have resumed office with effect from the forenoon of 22.08.05.

With regards

Yours sincerely,

(P.C.PARAKH)

Shri B.K.Chaturvedi,
Cabinet Secretary,
Cabinet Secretariate,
New Delhi.

Copy to : 1. MOS(C&M)
2. Shri T.K.A.Nair, Principal Secretary to PM.
3. Joint Secretary(Admn.), MOC.

(P.C.PARAKH)

Annexure 18-XII

Dharmendra Pradhan
Member of Parliament
(Lok Sabha)
Deogarh

Member :
- Standing Committee on Energy
- Petition Committee (Lok Sabha)

D.O.No.MP(LS)/DGH/05/ August 28, 2005

Respected Sir,

This has reference to the proceedings of the Consultative Committee of the Parliament of the Ministry of Coal held on 5.8.2005 wherein the subject of Coal India and its global competitiveness was under discussion. I would like to bring to your kind attention certain aspects of the said proceedings, which need to be addressed on an urgent basis.

(a) In his presentation of the subject of making Coal India globally competitive, the Chairman of Coal India stated, inter-alia, that the **CAG/CVC/CBI and the social objectives of the state are impediments to their functional autonomy.** Slide 29 of the said presentation (copy enclosed) is under reference in this regard. As Hon'ble Prime Minister is aware, the social objective of the state is the cardinal principle of planned economic development, which India has adopted since independence. In fact, the Nehruvian model of democratic socialism which the present government subscribes to is premised upon two basic objectives of **growth and social justice**. Public Sector Undertakings, which have been set up to fulfill the socialist objective of the Constitution, are mandated to subscribe to these fundamental principles. Consideration of the social objectives as an obstacle to their functional autonomy by Coal India is something which questions the very basics of our developmental model, and is, therefore, sacrilegious. **This is a serious matter, which arouses our sensitivity and sharp reaction. It is unbecoming of Coal India to make such a statement before the Committee and it is unfortunate that the concerned department of the Government allowed this presentation to be made, which is derogatory to the basic values and principles of our constitutional system.** Further, CAG is a constitutional authority who is mandated to play its role as a guardian of the public purse. Therefore, CAG is having jurisdiction over of Government Departments/Ministries and other Bodies like PSUs. To consider the CAG's and the

34, Meena Bagh, New Delhi - 110011 (Tel.: 011-23795212)
Handidhuan Chhak, Talcher, Distt. Angul, Orissa-759100 (Tel. : 06760-240234)

Dharmendra Pradhan
Member of Parliament
(Lok Sabha)
Deogarh

Member :
◦ Standing Committee on Energy
◦ Petition Committee (Lok Sabha)

-2-

CVC's jurisdiction as obstacle to Coal India's autonomy is to question the role and status of the constitutional authorities. Such irresponsible statements made by the Department and its PSU i.e. Coal India before a Parliamentary Committee, Hon'ble PM will agree, have grave implications for the state apparatus as well as for the time honoured public policies.

(b) Further, during the proceedings of the Consultative Committee, Secretary, Coal made certain statements in regard to the Action taken Report on the previous proceedings, which are contradicted by the facts. One such statement was that in Mahanadi Coalfields Limited (MCL), R&R Policy of the Govt. of Orissa is being implemented. Such a statement is far from truth and is misleading and amounts to misinformation to the Committee which is an august body of Parliament. The fact in the matter is that while the R&R policy of Govt. of Orissa is to provide employment to the land oustees for their rehabilitation, MCL has not provided any job in the last eight months to the land oustees and the claimants are more than 10,000. On the other hand, MCL, in their latest tender notice (copy enclosed) for three newly sanctioned projects, has indicated **outsourcing** of man power and machine. In the light of these facts, the undersigned as a Member of Committee contradicted the statement of the Secretary, Department of Coal and pointed out that the statement amounted to misinformation. **The Secretary's grievance that he was offended and humiliated should not make us miss out the substance of the matter, which is presentation of misinformation before the Committee and attempt to mislead the members**. Hon'ble Prime Minister may kindly appreciate that such an act of the part of no less a person than the Secretary to the Deptt. of Coal amounts to breach of privilege of the Committee and its members. In this regard it is pertinent to mention that in a Parliamentary system like ours, the ultimate responsibility to the people on any issue lies with the Members of Parliament, who are the representatives of the people. The Administrative authority must discharge their desired role of assisting the political executive in fulfillment of its responsibility to

34, Meena Bagh, New Delhi - 110011 (Tel.: 011-23795212)
Handidhuan Chhak, Talcher, Distt. Angul, Orissa-759100 (Tel. : 06760-240234)

Dharmendra Pradhan
Member of Parliament
(Lok Sabha)
Deogarh

Member :

- Standing Committee on Energy
- Petition Committee (Lok Sabha)

-3-

the people. Further, the Parliamentary system is based upon the principle of responsibility of executive to the legislature. In this case the Administrative Head of the Department i.e. the Secretary, who is the part of the executive organ of the Government, provides misleading information to the Parliamentary Committee which is a body of legislature. Such acts will certainly erode the fundamentals of the Parliamentary system and executive responsibility to legislature.

These are issues of deep concern having a bearing upon the well established practices of Parliamentary system and the constitutional arrangements made for the purpose. **Therefore, with all humility at my command, I appeal before the Hon'ble Prime Minister to address the real substance of the matter which is the central issue, rather than personal issues raised by the Secretary, Department of Coal which are peripheral in nature.**

With regards,

Yours sincerely,

(Dharmendra Pradhan)

Dr. Manmohan Singh,
Hon'ble Prime Minister
Government of India
New Delhi.

34, Meena Bagh, New Delhi - 110011 (Tel.: 011-23792812)
Handidhuan Chhak, Talcher, Distt. Angul, Orissa-759100 (Tel.: 06760-240234)

Annexure 18-XIII

No. 54012/4/2005-CA-II

Ministry of Coal
Government of India

New Delhi the 21st October, 2005

OFFICE MEMORANDUM

Subejct **Reference from PMO forwarding a copy of the letter dated 28.08.05 written by Shri Dharmendra Pradhan, MP regarding the proceedings of the Consultative Committee meeting held on 05.08.2005.**

The undersigned is directed to refer to PMO endorsement No. 200/31/C/63/2005-CS.I dated 09.05.2005 on the above subject and to state that the meeting of the Consultative Committee of the Ministry of Coal was held on 05.08.2005 with the agenda "Making Coal India Globally Competitive". The Minutes of the meeting have not yet been circulated. However, the position is clarified as follows:

1. **Presentation by Chairman, CIL**

i) During the course of the meeting, the Chairman of the Committee invited the Chairman, CIL to make a presentation to the Committee, as a prelude to initiating discussion and inviting suggestions from the members of the Committee on the subject matter chosen for agenda.

ii) The Chairman, CIL made a detailed presentation wherein he carried out a comprehensive analysis of emergence of CIL as a leader in coal industry, industry environment in the country, growth in coal production, technology adoption, cost of production, comparative study of performance of Indian coal industry vis-à-vis international trends, challenges and opportunities posed by international competition, major strengths and constraints in becoming globally competitive, efforts needed to be made by CIL, changes required in policy regimes and administrative framework etc.

iii) The presentation was in the nature of a SWOT analysis, wherein the Chief Executive of a public sector enterprise had sought to present, in a candid and transparent manner, the global business environment where its likely competitors seem to enjoy strategic advantages in terms of managerial practices. The Chairman, CIL, dwelt at length on several other issues such as capacity building, capacity utilization, quality improvement, efficient utilization of manpower and resources, likely scenario and steps required to be taken to effectively implement the mandate given to Coal India Limited in order to promote the energy security of the country. The thrust of the presentation was on securing qualitative improvements in the functioning of CIL.

iv) While discus ing the major constraints before CIL, the Chairman, CIL had sought to underline various factors such as legacy of the past, poor quality of indigenous equipments/spare parts, low utilisation of HEMM, socio-economic and socio-cultural factors, administrative and policy related issues etc. that might prove to be a handicap for the company in facing global competition. It was in that context that the Chairman, CIL had pointed out that being a Public Sector Enterprise (PSE), CIL was subject to the superintendence, regulation and control of various Constitutional and statutory authorities such as C&AG, CVC, CBI etc. This mandates adoption of practices and procedures that impose some limitations on the decision making processes. A PSE is also expected to subserve the socio-economic policy objectives of the Government, and to that extent, their decisions are not always guided or governed by purely commercial considerations. These remarks were meant to present an analysis of the strategic business environment in the public sector, which is not unique to CIL alone.

v) The Chairman, CIL had categorically clarified in the meeting itself that CIL was not seeking to exempt itself from the existing system of administrative or legislative scrutiny. He was only trying to make a realistic assessment of its strengths and constraints, so that limitations in CIL becoming globally competitive are clearly understood by the Members of Parliament.

vi) It may be mentioned that various Committees set up by the Government, including the recent Sengupta Committee, have recommended grant of greater functional autonomy to PSEs in the context of the changed liberalised economic environment. And the Central Government have taken many initiatives recently in this regard. There was nothing in the presentation of Chairman, CIL which can be called derogatory to the basic principles of our constitutional system or sacrilegious. The Consultative Committee of Parliament is meant for a free and frank discussion and Chairman, CIL has full right to express his views and need not be constrained by the views of the Secretary or the Minister. There is, therefore, no reason as to why either Secretary or MOS(C&M) should have restrained Chairman, CIL from expressing his views candidly.

2. **<u>R&R Policy</u>**

i) The Hon'ble Member (Shri D. Pradhan), during his intervention, stated that the Secretary (Coal) had made public statements on R&R Policy of CIL during his recent visit to Orissa, after his meetings with the Chief Minister and the Chief Secretary of the State. The Chairman, Consultative Committee had asked Secretary (Coal) to clarify the position.

ii) Secretary (Coal) stated that during his discussions with the Chief Minister as well as the Chief Secretary of Orissa, he had highlighted the policy approach followed by CIL in regard to resettlement and rehabilitation. CIL has an R&R Policy that provides for employment to land-oustees subject to availability of vacancies, and actual need for additional manpower. In case employment cannot be given, cash compensation is given in lieu of employment. He stated that in a large number of projects, lands were acquired and employment provided by the coal companies in contravention of the provisions of the R&R Policy. CCL, BCCL & ECL, in particular, continued to provide employment even though they already had surplus manpower. Adequate monetary compensation is given for land as well as rehabilitation of land-losers. Over and above that if employment is to be given to people who cannot be gainfully employed by the coal companies, it would be impossible for CIL to become globally competitive. The coal companies would, however, continue to provide employment to land-oustees to the extent feasible and permitted under the provisions of the R&R Policy of CIL. The Secretary (Coal) informed that his contention was appreciated by the Chief Minister and the Chief Secretary of Orissa. They also mentioned that they were reviewing the State R&R Policy.

(iii) There was no misinformation in the statement of Secretary (Coal). He clearly stated what was discussed by him with the Chief Secretary and the Chief Minister of Orissa. There was nothing in the statement of the Secret ary that can be termed 'misinformation' or 'misleading'.

(iv) If the Hon'ble Member felt that statement of Secretary (Coal) amounted to breach of 'privilege of the Committee', he had full right to take up the matter with the Privilege Committee of the House. But, he had no right to use insulting language against the Secretary. We are a democracy and every citizen, which includes civil servants of all ranks, has a right to live with dignity and self respect. Our Constitution does not give any right to Members of Parliament to insult its citizens or use derogatory language against them. In fact, the Hon'ble Member is guilty of breach of privilege of the House, by conducting himself in a manner unbecoming of a Member of the August House. Members of Parliament occupy a very important position in our Constitutional democracy and are expected to conduct themselves with dignity and decorum expected of such high offices. The Government and the Speaker of the Lok Sabha should take note of this so that such unfortunate incidents do not happen in future.

v) It is unfortunate that the Hon'ble Member does not place any value on self respect and dignity of fellow citizens. Instead of expressing regret for the unbecoming conduct, he is trying to justify his conduct on totally untenable grounds.

This has the approval of the Secretary (Coal).

(Rakesh Sharma)

Under Secretary to the Govt. of India

To

The Prime Minister Office
(Kind attention Shri K.V. Pratap, Deputy Secretary)
South Block, New Delhi.

Annexure 19-I

PERSONAL & CONFIDENTIAL 1-5

शिबू सोरेन
SHIBU SOREN

कोयला मंत्री
भारत सरकार
नई दिल्ली–110 001
MINISTER OF COAL
GOVERNMENT OF INDIA
NEW DELHI-110 001

7th February, 2005

Hon'ble Prime Minister Sri Manmohan Singh ji,

My Secretary (Coal) has a style of functioning that has no blend of procedure, harmony and respect for political leadership. To his convinces, he flounders rules of business executive working with the intention of by- passing the Ministers. His recent conduct represents procedural failure and gross insubordination. He presumes that I am simple and gullible tribal and, therefore, he can behave in such an irresponsible manner.

I recount some instances below to further substantiate the point, mentioned by me:

i) When I first took the charge of Coal & Mines Ministry in May 2004, I had sent a note to the Secretary of Coal to provide me with inputs to formulate new coal policy. While doing so, I had clearly mentioned that this should be submitted on time bound basis as I would want this to be announced by the Hon'ble Prime Minister as a part of his address to the nation from Red Fort on 15th August 2004. The Secretary (Coal) failed to even attempt this.

ii) At the same time, I sent another note to the Secretary asking him necessary information to deal with coal mafia. The Secretary did not give me required information nor he could explain to me delay in submitting the same. As a matter of fact, required information are not furnished to me till now which is a deliberate attempt to hide information from a Cabinet Minister. You will please agree with me that this is a serious lapse on the part of the Secretary besides being an absolute act of disobedience.

iii) In May 2004 immediately on taking over the Ministry, I discussed the issue of appointing regular CMD of Coal India Limited with the Secretary. NDA Government had suspended N.K.Sharma, then CMD of CIL overnight. I had called this file to know the details. Before I could form any opinion, one day the file of dismissal of N.K.Sharma was put up to me and my signature were taken

....2/-

4-6

शिबू सोरेन
SHIBU SOREN

कोयला मंत्री
भारत सरकार
नई दिल्ली–110 001
MINISTER OF COAL
GOVERNMENT OF INDIA
NEW DELHI-110 001

-:: 2 ::-

telling me all kind of urgency. Incidentally, immediately I received a letter from an Hon'ble M.P. complaining about conspired dismissal of N.K.Sharma. This letter was forwarded to the Secretary asking his explanation. You will be surprised to note that this letter was suppressed and once again the Secretary indulged into act of insubordination. The file of N.K.Sharma is now resubmitted to me. The conspired approach of the Secretary speaks volumes of his strategy to install NDA and coal lobby sponsored Shashi Kumar as the C.M.D. of Coal India Limited. The sequence of events of last nine months does represent this.

iv) *The Secretary, for the reasons best known to him, did not start the process of appointing a regular C.M.D. of CIL during my last stay as the Cabinet Minister. He initiated the process after my leaving the Ministry. The process, thus started by the Secretary, had only one objective and that was to appoint Shashi Kumar as the regular C.M.D. of CIL, over looking and relaxing many norms. I had been reading about this in various newspapers. The rumour was that the Secretary wants to have Shashi Kumar as the regular C.M.D. of CIL, before my taking the oath of Minister for the second time. The pressure was also exerted on the Hon'ble Minister of State (Coal & Mines).*

v) *As soon as I took the oath in December 2004 as the Cabinet Minister of Coal, in respect of the proposal for appointment of regular CMD of the Coal India Ltd., I have come to notice certain glaring inadequacies in the way the Secretary has handled the issue. While putting up the proposal for the approval of the Minister of Coal, he has disregarded the first recommendation of the CVC which required the Department to look into the issue of certain Directors of the Board of CIL being guilty of non-application of mind in the matter of unauthorized procurement of explosives worth about Rs. 300 crores. (The then CMD is under suspension and facing major disciplinary proceedings for the same).*

शिबू सोरेन
SHIBU SOREN

कोयला मंत्री
भारत सरकार
नई दिल्ली–110 001
MINISTER OF COAL
GOVERNMENT OF INDIA
NEW DELHI-110 001

-:: 3 ::-

vi) *When the same was pointed out, the file was resubmitted without the necessary enquiry reports, records and views of the Department in the matter. All that was said was that the CVC has subsequently withdrawn their reference and hence the proposal may be approved. It was expected of the Secretary to have provided all the necessary records and documents when the substantial issue was raised regarding the role of a Director who was recommended for appointment as a regular CMD of CIL. I find this as a serious intentional lapse, which is unacceptable, as the same is not expected of the Secretary.*

vii) *When the Department's proposal for appointment of the first candidate on the panel recommended by the PESB for appointment as CMD of CIL was rejected by me, I expected the Secretary to again put up the file to me for appointing the second candidate in the panel for the said post. However, without my knowledge, the Secretary (Coal) has decided, on his own, to send the file to ACC. This is absolute failure on the part of the Secretary to follow the procedure and business rules. This shows that the Secretary does not bother about the only Adivasi Minister in the Cabinet. He considers himself to be superior to the Cabinet Minister and Minister of State (Coal). The attitude of the Secretary on this issue represents his obsession to appoint Shashi Kumar as the CMD of CIL for the reasons best known to him.*

viii) *Malafide intention and motive of the Secretary to pave way for the appointment of Shashi Kumar are obvious.*

ix) *There was lots of discussion about the motives of the Secretary in the coal trade. Immediately on my taking over as the Minister of Coal, the MPs requested me to investigate. I received written complaints from them too.*

.....4/-

1-8

शिबू सोरेन
SHIBU SOREN

कोयला मंत्री
भारत सरकार
नई दिल्ली–110 001
MINISTER OF COAL
GOVERNMENT OF INDIA
NEW DELHI-110 001

-:: 4 ::-

x) *The Department has not demonstrated the desired sense of urgency in allocating long-term linkages that are vital for various projects to take off. The Standing Linkage Committee, which does this job, did not meet for more than one year and a half. When such meeting was finally held, it was without the necessary preparatory work, resulting in no substantial outcome. At the time, when coal availability is so critical this only represents lack of understanding of external environment which has complete dependence on distribution of coal.*

xi) *With regard to the mechanism of allocating captive coal blocks, while the entire range of industry, including their administrative Ministries, was opposed to captive bidding for various reasons, the Secretary (Coal) preferred to misled as if the industry was in favour of it.*

xii) *I have noticed a certain tendency of inaction in the name of proposed policy changes. While new policy initiatives meant for positive gains are welcome, presenting it as an alibi to defer decisions is difficult to appreciate. Critical sectors of the economy like Power, Iron, Steel and Cement are so dependent on coal that delay in its availability will have adverse consequences on economic growth. These sectors were made to feel the pinch for a considerable period of time on account of inaction by the Department.*

xiii) *As a Minister of Coal, my priorities are new coal policy, employment in coal rich areas like Jharkhand and rehabilitation etc. But, the Secretary (Coal) has priority focused on only e-auction. The Hon'ble Prime Minister as Minister of Coal has approved only a Pilot Project for e-auction of coal in BCCL with specific reference to only 1.60 lakh tons of coal. Only one trial e-auction has been conducted so far. The Secretary (Coal) has, however, permitted BCCL to put the entire non-core sector coal and the entire production of North Eastern coalfields to be supplied through e-auction without my approval. He has done so despite my saying that this proposal needs to be properly addressed after adequate feed back from sufficient trial auctions in order to achieve objectives of coal distribution rather encouraging indirect monopoly in coal trade and lose control on its end user pricing.*

.....5/-

शिबू सोरेन
SHIBU SOREN

कोयला मंत्री
भारत सरकार
नई दिल्ली–110 001
MINISTER OF COAL
GOVERNMENT OF INDIA
NEW DELHI-110 001

-:: 5 ::-

xiv) *The worse is that even as Cabinet Ministers are prevented from going public on policy matters before they are duly decided by the government, Secretary (Coal) and, at his behest, some CMDs have announced that e-auction would soon be implemented all over Coal India Ltd. This is nothing but pressurizing the Government into accepting something which is not considered in details. In the end, if a contrary view is to be taken based on results of e-auction trials, the Minister and the Government would be seen as anti reform. I am already concerned by the feed back in respect of e-auction.*

xv) *Effective functioning of PSUs is one of the main concerns of the Hon'ble Prime Minister. The administrative departments are expected to discharge their role effectively in the monitoring of the performance of Board level functionaries within the existing parameters. It has come to my notice that the Department of Coal has taken a long period of one to two years in processing the proposals for regularization of appointment of Board level functionaries. As a consequence, some of them would have continued without due regularization and may have even retired so. A file was put up to the Minister for regularizing the appointment of 10 Board level functionaries without the much-desired Special Performance Appraisal Reports. The Secretary (Coal) was asked to resubmit the said file, duly completing SPARs, the same was not done for about three months now.*

xvi) *Lack of consistency is another area of concern. With the due approval of Hon'ble Prime Minister as Minister of Coal, a series of Screening Committee meetings under the Chairmanship of Secretary (Coal) are being held for allocation of captive coal blocks to various sectors of the industry. Before the first meeting, the Secretary (Coal) should have recommended and got approved the parameters of such allocation. It has been brought to my notice that half way through he is preferring to change the quantum and period of allocation which is being resented by the industry. This kind of approach may not reflect positively on the style of functioning of the government.*

....6/-

50

शिबू सोरेन
SHIBU SOREN

कोयला मंत्री
भारत सरकार
नई दिल्ली–110 001
MINISTER OF COAL
GOVERNMENT OF INDIA
NEW DELHI-110 001

-:: 6 ::-

xvii) *Allocation of captive coal blocks and long term and short term coal linkages are one of the core areas of the functioning of the Department of Coal. Surprisingly, Minister of Coal was being kept out of the loop in this regard for the reasons best known to Secretary (Coal). In respect of these two issues, representatives of industry and Hon'ble Members of Parliament keep representing substantial issues concerning the methodology, criteria, priorities etc. to the Minister of Coal. To be kept abreast of all these matters, I had desired to be associated with the same by putting up the minutes of the Committee meetings to me. The Secretary (Coal) has only reluctantly agreed to it demonstrating his lack of faith in the political leadership that is supposed to be pivotal in the Cabinet System of Governance. The Secretary (Coal), I conclude, does consider me as an untouchable and brainless in the context of providing of information to his Cabinet Minister.*

xviii) *The Department has proposed creation of a special fund for parking the stowing excise duty receipts for the purpose of carrying out statutory functions relating to safety in the mines, development of infrastructure etc. This is a major initiative and the Secretary has gone ahead with the same without my knowledge and approval. As I am fully aware of the problems related to coal areas, I had asked the Secretary (Coal) to work on development of infrastructure and rehabilitation process under Coal Area Development Body and submit blue print so that the same could have been discussed with you. The idea was to get appropriate approval and you could have announced the same during your 2004 speech of 15th August from Red Fort. Once again, Secretary (Coal) failed in carrying out instructions.*

xix) *Secretary (Coal) had recently been on a foreign visit with deviation in the tour programme approved by the Hon'ble Prime Minister in the capacity of Minister of Coal. The revised tour programme was to be submitted for approval of the competent authority. He has not done so, for a considerable period of time, setting a bad example. The concerned section has noted in the file that the Secretary's office has not given the revised tour programme despite reminders.*

.....7/-

51

शिबू सोरेन
SHIBU SOREN

कोयला मंत्री
भारत सरकार
नई दिल्ली–110 001
MINISTER OF COAL
GOVERNMENT OF INDIA
NEW DELHI-110 001

-:: 7 ::-

xx) *In the meantime, there were complaints of the Secretary (Coal) visiting Switzerland without due approval. Had he submitted the tour programme within the time, the controvery could have been avoided.*

xxi) *To cap it all, the Secretary (Coal) does not seem to be having due regard to the political leadership. It has been reported to me by reliable sources that he has been making uncharitable comments about me amounting to questioning the wisdom of the Hon'ble Prime Minister in my appointment as Minister of Coal.*

In view of the above, I have to reluctantly take a view that it may not be appropriate to continue any further with the present Secretary (Coal). I, hence request the Hon'ble Prime Minister to kindly consider to substitute the present incumbent with a suitable alternative.

The Secretary (Coal) is an appointee of Chandra Babu Naidu, during NDA Government. I normally overlook political leaning of the officers working in the Ministry. But, I feel that even a Secretary can work to create a rift in UPA. I do feel that the Secretaries working in the Centre do not care about Adivasi Ministers. Please understand my feelings and change the present Secretary (Coal) immediately. As also, please take administrative action against him for insubordination and failure to follow business rules intentionally.

With regards,

Yours sincerely,

(Shibu Soren)

Dr. Manmohan Singh,
Hon'ble Prime Minister of India,
7, Race Course Road,
New Delhi.

Annexure 19-II

राष्ट्रीय प्रतीक

P.C. PARAKH
SECRETARY

भारत सरकार
कोयला मंत्रालय
शास्त्री भवन, नई दिल्ली–110001
Government of India
Ministry of Coal
Shastri Bhawan, New Delhi-11000

Telephone : 23384884
Fax : 23381678

Confidential

No. 28/S/Secy(Coal) 22nd March, 2005

Dear Shri Chaturvedi,

Kindly refer to your D.O. letter No. 10/7/2005-CS(A) dated 12/2/05. As desired my comments on the note are enclosed.

There is no gainsaying that I have had difference of opinion with both Minister of State and Cabinet Minister on several issues of policy and administration. I have found nothing of substance in the note for which I can be faulted. I have explained my position on each of the issues raised by the Minister.

In my understanding I have performed my duties in the manner that is expected of a member of Civil Service. As Secretary to the Government, I am deeply conscious of the fact that I cannot effectively discharge my responsibilities without full political support from my Ministers. However, I am at loss to understand as to what could be done.

With regards

Yours sincerely,

(P.C. Parakh)

Encl: as above

Shri B.K. Chaturvedi,
Cabinet Secretary,
Cabinet Secretariat,
Rashtrapati Bhawan,
New Delhi-4.

Comments on the note enclosed with the D.O. letter No.10/7/2005-CS(A) dated 12th February, 2005 from Cabinet Secretary

Before giving my comments on each para of the note, I would like to make brief comments on the introductory para which states " Secretary (Coal) has a style of functioning that he has no respect for political leadership by-passing the Minister as in following instances"

Entire five page note, does not refer to a single instance where I have by-passed the Ministers or not implemented any written orders issued by the them. I have always been polite and courteous in my written and oral communications with the Ministers and complied with all written orders even when I had serious of difference of opinion.

However, if respect for political leadership implies compiling with oral orders or recording notings that suits Minister's interest, as against public interest, I am perhaps guilty of alleged short-comings.

Ministers perhaps do not appreciate that Business Rules of the Government of India confer certain rights and enjoin certain responsibilities on the Secretary to the Government. As Secretary to the Government , I have both the right and responsibility to advise the Minister as to what I consider rational, fair and in public interest. It is, of course, for the Minister to accept or reject such advice.

While note does not quote any instance of my by-passing Minister's orders, I would like to quote a few instances where I promptly complied with written orders, which were against my advice and which I consider were wrong, partisan and against public interest, duly respecting right of the Minister to reject my advice.

-2-

(i) CBI had requested for registering a regular case against Shri M K. Thapar, CMD, SECL under Section 120(B) read with Section 420 of IPC and Section 13(2) read with Section 13(1)(d) of Prevention of Corruption Act. After examining the material of record, file was submitted to PM as Minister (Coal) through MOS(C&M)) with the recommendation to permit CBI to register the case. PM directed me to give a hearing to the officers concerned and submit a self-contained note taking all aspects of the matter into consideration. Accordingly, I visited Ranchi, examined all the relevant documents as well as officers concerned and found that there was more than an adequate evidence of misconduct on the part of Shri M.K. Thapar. I, therefore, recommended that CBI may be permitted to register a regular case. Ministers did not agree with the advice. However, orders of Ministers were compiled with though I consider it was a wrong order. It is a different matter that the said orders has since been revised by the Prime Minister as Minister in-charge of the Coal Ministry.

(ii) Minister (Coal) has desired that Shri B. Bhattacharya, Director (Technical), CMPDIL should be transferred to BCCL vice Shri H.R. Surana, Director (Technical), BCCL. It was suggested to the Minister that Mr. Surana was due to retire in couple of months and it is not desirable to shift Directors from one company to another, unless there are compelling reasons to do so. It may be noted that powers of inter-company transfer of Directors was extensively misused in this Ministry for reasons which are not difficult to understand and hence these powers were withdrawn from Ministry by ACC. In compliance with written orders of the Minister proposals were sent to ACC. ACC, of course did not approve the proposal. Requests for several more transfer of Directors were orally made by the Minister, which I had politely declined to recommend.

-3-

(iii) Screening Committee consisting of representatives of various Ministries has been deliberating and deciding allocation of captive Coal mining blocks for the last several years. Agenda notes and minutes of these meetings were never submitted for approval of the Minister. Minister, however, desired that agenda notes and minutes of meeting should be submitted to him. Approval of agenda notes and minutes by Minister does not serve any useful purpose. In fact, it is a strange request that the minutes of the meetings to which Minister is not a party should be approved by him. However, orders of the Minister were promptly complied with.

These are the few instances of orders which were irrational and not in public interest, but have been compiled with, duly respecting the right of the Minister to reject advice tendered by the Secretary.

I would now proceed to deal with each of the paras of the note:

(i) A copy of the note dated 18.06.04 received from Shri Shibu Soren soon after he took charge as Minister of Coal & Mines is placed at Annexure-I. The information sought by the Minister in his note was made available and file submitted to him on 14.07.04 It was also orally informed to the Minister that none of the policy initiatives that could be taken by Coal Ministry would of such relevance to common masses to deserve reference by the Prime Minister in his Independence Day address from ramparts of the Red Fort. The file was received back in the office on 26.07.04 without any comments after the Minister demitted his office.

However, a number of policy initiatives have been taken by the Ministry. Some of these have been implemented and some could not be implemented because of unwillingness on the part of the Minister to bring about required transparency in respect

-4-

of some of the policies. Some of the major policy initiatives taken by the Department are:-

a) Allocation of captive Coal blocks through open competitive bidding.

b) Marketing of Coal through internet based e-auction.

c) Out-sourcing of mining activities in Coal India for greater efficiency and economy.

d) Allocation of Coal blocks to public sector power utilities and State Government companies on par with CIL.

e) Allocation of Coal blocks on group captive basis and leader associate basis.

f) Conferring status of Mini-Ratna to Coal companies in order to enable them to have greater delegation of powers.

g) Streamlining process of project approvals

(ii) As regards dealing with Coal mafia, Minister perhaps has far more knowledge about operations and strength of Coal mafia as he comes from a State where strangle hold of the Coal mafia is strongest. Coal mafia is not outside the Government. It exists within the Ministry of Coal, Coal companies , trade unions, State administrations and local political leadership. There are no easy and short cut solutions to the problem of Coal mafia in the current political and administrative milieu of the country. Dealing with Coal mafia requires strong political commitment at Central and State Government level and ability to effectively enforce Law and Order which does not exist. I had no solution to offer to the Minister apart from bringing about structural changes in the operations of Coal industry for which Ministers have shown great reluctance.

-5-

(iii) to (viii) All these paras relate to appointment of regular CMD for CIL. Shri NK Sharma, the then CMD, CIL was placed under suspension by the Government on 4/6/03. Proposals for termination of services of Shri NK Sharma or in the alternative creation of super-numerary post in order to fill up the post of CMD, CIL on regular basis were initiated by my predecessor well before I took charge of the Ministry. By the time I took charge of the Ministry, the post of CMD, CIL had already remained vacant for over nine months. CIL is too important for country's energy sector to remain without a regular Head for a long time. I, therefore, followed up both the proposal in order to see that post of CMD, CIL is filled up on regular basis at the earliest. I did seek and obtain approval of Minister for termination of services of Shri NK Sharma as E.O. required fresh approval from the new Minister. After proposal had been sent to the E.O. Minister endorsed to recall the proposal on receipt of a letter from Shri Tek Lal Mahto, MP. I advised the Minister that having once sent the proposal in respect of an officer who is facing several charges of misconduct, it will not be appropriate for him to recall the proposal, and the Minister agreed with the advice.

Though proposals for termination of Shri Sharma and/or creation of a supernumerary post in the grade of Chairman CIL were being constantly followed up. Orders for creation of supernumerary posts were received from PMO only after Shri Soren had resigned. While creating of supernumerary post, PM also directed to fill up the post of CMD, CIL within one month. Accordingly process of selection was expedited and completed by the time Shri Soren was re-inducted in the Cabinet. I could not have had premonition about resignation and re-induction of Shri Soren to conspire and get Mr. Shashi Kumar selected in the intervening period. In any case selection for appointment of CMD was made by PESB and not me.

-6-

After post of CMD, CIL was notified by PESB, it was found that Mr. Shashi Kumar was the only candidate within CIL who fulfilled the criteria for selection. It was, therefore, considered necessary to relax minimum experience required in order to see that PESB has a reasonable number of candidates from whom to select CMD , CIL. This was done in consultation with PESB. Relaxation in qualifying experience was not given in favour of Shri Shashi Kumar, but in favour of other officers. This can in no way be considered as a favour shown to Shri Shashi Kumar.

As regards alleged involvement of Shri Shashi Kumar in purchase of explosives for which Mr. N K Sharma was suspended, the relevant facts were in the knowledge of CVC and I am sure CVC would have taken note of these facts while giving vigilance clearance in respect of Shri Shashi Kumar. However, in view of the reservations expressed by the MOS, the role of Shri Shashi Kumar was fully investigation by CVO, CIL and CVC after examining the report of CVO, CIL has rightly advised that there was no misconduct on the part of Shri Shashi Kumar in purchase of explosives.

After second clearance from CVC in respect of Shri Shashi Kumar was received, file for the appointment of Shri Shashi Kumar was submitted with the direction to the Joint Secretary that the file in which CVC's clearance was received may also be submitted separately to the Minister for his perusal. The reason for processing both the files simultaneously was to ensure that there is no further delay in processing proposal for appointment of CMD, CIL and not to hold back any information from the Minister.

When the file for appointment of Shri Shashi Kumar was submitted for approval, it was clearly recorded in the note that the second candidate in the panel recommended by PESB was Shri V.K. Singh who was also clear from vigilance angle. If Minister had preference for Shri V.K. Singh, he could have indicated his preference for Shri V K Singh, while rejecting the proposal for appointment of Shri Shashi Kumar.

-7-

It is clearly laid down in the Transaction of Business Rules of the Government of India that the decision on acceptance or rejection of recommendation of PESB has to be taken by Appointment Committee of Cabinet(ACC) of which Minister is a member. In order to enable ACC to take a decision in the matter, all facts including detailed notings of the Minister have been communicated to ACC. In my understanding of the Business Rules, this is the only way in which cases where Minister differ from the recommendation of PESB have to be processed.

I hold Mr. Shibu Soren in great esteem as a popular tribal leader. Difference of opinion on specific issues does not mean that I do not bother for the only Advasi Minister.

I have seen working of Shri Shashi Kumar for the last one year. Shri Kumar is one of the few officers in Coal industry with impeachable record of personal and professional integrity and courage of conviction. It will be great injustice if his name for posting as CMD, CIL is rejected on extraneous considerations.

The decision of Coal Ministry to reject request of CBI to register a case against Shri Thapar and efforts to some how find some evidence of misconduct against Shri Kumar can not but send a message to the executives in CIL that personal and professional integrity does not matter and officers with resources or right connection can get away with anything. This will be a very unfortunate message to convey to an industry which is rampant with corruption and fully under control of mafia.

(ix) I am not aware of any discussions about my motives in the Coal trade as nothing specific has been mentioned about in the note. It is therefore not possible to make any comment on this observation.

-8-

As regards complaints from Members of Parliaments, lesser said the better. I had heard that signatures of MPs can be obtained for a price on any piece of paper. I wish it was not true. However, my experience of working in the Ministry for last one year makes me believe that it is unfortunately true. I had earlier in my D.O. letter No. Secy(C)/3.01.05 dated 6.12.04 had brought to the notice of Cabinet Secretariat false and baseless allegation levelled against me by Shri Chandra Sekhar Dubey, MP from Dhanbad. I had requested Cabinet Secretary to bring this matter to the notice of PM and Speaker of Lok Sabha for appropriate action. I am not aware if Government has taken any action on that letter.

Subsequent to Shri C.S. Dubey's letter , another complaint against me was made by Shri Giridhar Yadav. I was very hurt by these motivated complaints from MPs and I had decided to call it a day and seek retirement from the Service. I had in fact drafted a letter which on second thought I did not send to you. I am attaching a copy of this draft as Annexure-2.

I am sorry to say that the Members of Indian Parliament who swear to uphold the Constitution of India can with impunity indulge in black mailing civil servants and senior executives of public sector companies to meet their personal ends. It is unfortunate that country has no institutional mechanism to stop such misconduct on the part of the law makers.

(x) As regards the allegation that Standing Linkage Committee(SLC) has not met for last more than one and half year, the responsibility does not lie on my door. I had been Secretary of the Department for less than one year. SLC meeting was scheduled in the month of April, 2004 soon after my taking charge but had to be postponed on the Directives of the then Minister (Coal) Ms. Mamta Banerjee, who wanted the meeting to be held only after elections to Parliament.

-9-

In any case with the current negative Coal balance, there is hardly any scope for giving new linkages. Any additional linkages without increasing production can be only a theoretical exercise.

(xi) As regards allocation of captive Coal blocks through competitive bidding, there are opinions in favour and against it. However, there can be no doubt that such a system will be far more transparent than any system that is based on subjective considerations. While both MOS and M(Coal) were strongly opposed to the idea, Prime Minister as Minister (Coal) had approved the proposal. I did not make any misrepresentation on the issue and deliberations of the meeting with stake holders were faithfully recorded.

(xii) This perhaps refers to non allocation of captive Coal blocks pending approval of new policy of allocation based on competitive bidding. I did not expect that this proposal which will bring total transparency in allocation of Coal Block would face so many hurdles. Even after Prime Minister while holding charge as Minister (Coal) had approved the proposal, Cabinet Note could not be processed as file remained pending with the Minister till he second time demitted the office. However, based on the decision given by Prime Minister to continue the present system of allocation, pending introduction of competitive bidding , five Screening Committee meetings were held in the last four months and decisions has been taken in respect of more companies in last few months than what was done in the previous 10 years.

(xiii) No new Coal policy can create additional employment in sick Coal companies of Jharkhand which are already incurring losses because of huge unproductive manpower.

-10-

MOS and M(Coal) were always opposed to the e-auction proposal. Prime Minister during the short spell as Minister in-charge of Coal Ministry, approved a trial e-auction. Trial e-auction was conducted successfully and netted substantial additional revenue for BCCL. Once the first trial auction was successful, it was logical to extend it further and have some more trials in order to frame new marketing policy. However, Minister kept the file pending and finally before resignation rejected the proposal without indicating any reasons. Dy. Chairman, Planning Commission has also recommended marketing of Coal through e-auction and the proposal has now been resubmitted for the approval of Prime Minister in his capacity as M(Coal).

There is large scale of black marketing and generation of black money through patronage of Coal mafia in current system of marketing of Coal. In trial e-auction at NEC premium received was as high as Rs. 1000/ per tonne amounting to Rs. 25 lakhs per rake. Instead of this revenue legitimately accruing to the Coal companies which have been incurring losses year after year, this is being cornered by the black marketeers and mafia. The Minister instead of supporting the efforts of CMD, CIL to curb malpractices has been standing in the way of bringing transparency in marketing operations.

(xiv) There is nothing wrong in CMD CIL going to the press and announcing that if successful, trial e-auction will be extended to other companies also. In fact a public debate is a part of process of policy formation. Reaction generated through such public communications help in re-defining and fine tuning public policy. Transparency in Coal marketing is prime need of the Coal industry and will be one major steps towards curbing role of Coal mafia.

-11-

(xv) Responsibilities for delay of more than two years in confirmation of Board level appointees can not be that of a Secretary who has been in office for less than one year. In fact all the pending case were submitted for confirmation after my taking over as Coal Secretary. File for regularization was submitted based on the recommendation of PESB. PESB makes its recommendation based on the SPAR and lapse on the part of officers in not linking SPAR is not such a serious matter for which Minister should find faults with the Secretary.

(xvi) Screening Committee in recent meetings have proposed Group Captive Mining, concept of leader and associates, reduced period of mine life etc. These policy changes have been generally welcomed by the applicants for captive blocks and will result in significant improvement in satisfaction of Coal demand in the shortest possible time . No policy can be valid for indefinite time, and has to constantly evolve based on the felt needs of the society. These changes in policy came out of deliberation of Screening Committee and have been submitted for the approval of the Minister. Any change in policy may adversely affect interests of some individuals, who may oppose it. But a policy formulated in larger public interest can not be faulted on account of opposition of a few.

(xvii) Allocation of captive Coal blocks has been going on for last 10 years and Long Term Coal linkages are being given ever since Nationalisation of Coal Industry. These decisions have always been taken by the Screening Committee and Standing Committee that are inter-ministerial forums for decision making. Agenda and minutes of these meetings were not being approved by the Ministers. This practice was not started by me, I can not therefore be blamed for keeping Minister out of loop.

-12-

There is no merit in approval of agenda notes and minutes of meetings of these Committees by the Minister (Coal). If these committees suggest any policy change certainly those need approval of the Minister. But every decision taken by these inter-ministerial Committee does not need approval of the Minister. Such concentration of powers which is anti thesis of declared policy of the Government for greater delegation and decentralisation of powers. Since I did not find any merit in prior approval of agenda notes and minutes of meeting of these Committees, I had recorded my views against this proposal . However, agenda items and minutes of these meetings are now being submitted for approval of the Minister.

I have always candidly recorded my views on all proposals and promptly compiled with written orders even where my advice has not been accepted by the Minister. A difference of opinion can not be construed as reluctance to comply with orders or lack of faith in political leadership.

(xviii) Stowing exercise duty is collected and credited to general revenues of the Union . Under Law , this duty is levied for development of infrastructure and taking measures for conservation of Coal and safety in Coal mining areas. Since these funds are credited to general revenues, a proposal was made to the Finance Ministry to credit these amounts in a separate fund so that amount collected as stowing exercise duty are available exclusively for the purpose mandated by Law This was only an administrative change suggested in the interest of proper utilisation of fund. The file was submitted to the Minister for information after sending the proposal to the Finance Ministry. Minister has not found fault into the proposal. I am unable to see what is the issue about.

A suggestion was made by the Minister for creation of Coal Area Development Authority by crediting 1% of the profits of Coal Companies in a special fund. Such a fund can be created only by enacting a Law. This proposal has serious implications not only for Coal industry but also for other sectors of Economy as similar demand can be made for creation of funds for Petroleum sector, Power sector and so on.

-13-

Pending formation of such an Authority it was suggested to the Minister that Public Sector Coal companies can contribute Rs. 1/- per tonne of Coal produced to be used for creation of fund for peripheral development of Coal bearing areas. A scheme was accordingly drafted in consultation with CIL when the file was put to the Minister he suggested Rs. 2/- per tonne should be collected for to the fund. The proposal has therefore been again referred to CIL for its views.

(xix) & (xx) My tour programme for visit to US and Spain was approved by the PM as Minister (Coal). However, before the tour was undertaken it was found that Spain leg may not be useful in view of absence of senior executives of M/s Miscelin who were otherwise occupied. The programme was, therefore, was slightly modified to drop Spain and include visit to two factories where hydraulic Coal mining equipment are manufacturing. These two factories are located in close proximity of Frankfurt which has to be any way touched on way to US. In the absence of PM who was Minister-in-charge of Coal and was on US tour, revised tour programme was got approved by the MOS. The revised tour did not result in any additional expenditure for the Government and in fact resulted in considerable savings. I am unable to understand as to why delay in ratification of revised tour programme which was approved by the MOS should be made into an issue.

(xxi) I had never made any uncharitable remarks about MOS or Coal Minister despite my serious differences with them on several policy issues.

As regards respect for political leadership. I have already dealt with it in my introductory remarks.

CONFIDENTIAL

No.10/7/2005-CS(A)
CABINET SECRETARIAT

In his letter dated 8th August, Shri P C Parakh, IAS(AP:69) has pointed out the unfortunate conduct of Shri Dharmendra Pradhan, Member of Parliament, vis-à-vis Shri Parakh, in the course of the meeting of the Consultative Committee of the Members of Parliament attached to the Ministry of Coal, on 5th August, 2005. Shri Parakh has given notice of voluntary retirement, and mentioned that he is proceeding on earned leave w.e.f.9th August, 2005. He is superannuating on 31st December, 2005.

2. It was only recently that Shri C S Dubey, Member of Parliament, had made a number of allegations against Shri Parakh. The allegations, and also, a complaint from the then Coal Minister was examined in detail, after taking into account the comments of the officer himself. None of the allegations against Shri Parakh were found to be proved and Prime Minister had approved that the matter be closed.

3. I have talked to Shri Parakh to reassure him of our full support in his efforts to meet the challenges of the Coal sector including determination to fight the Coal mafia. I have also assured him that the Government has full faith in his stewardship as Secretary of the Coal Ministry, and that the matter will be brought to the notice of the Prime Minister. We have to keep in mind that such incidents do not happen and proceedings in these Committees are civil. I understand that Shri Parakh is likely to resume duties from Tuesday, 16th August, 2005.

4. It maybe appropriate if informally this is brought to the notice of the Speaker.

(B K Chaturvedi)
Cabinet Secretary
13-08-2005

PRIME MINISTER

Sudhir Mungantiwar
Member of Legislative Assembly
Ex Cabinet Minister (Maharashtra)

दिनांक : २४.९.२००५

प्रति,

मा. श्री. पारिख साहब
सचिव,
केंद्रीय कोयला मंत्रालय,
भारत सरकार, नई दिल्ली.

सप्रेम जय विदर्भ !

महोदय,

आपसे मेरी प्रत्यक्ष मुलाकात नहीं हुयी है, लेकिन मैंने आपके बारेमें, आपकी प्रामाणिकताके बारेमें बहुत सुना है इसलिये यह पत्र आपके प्रती अपनी भावनाएँ उजागर करने हेतु लिख रहा हूँ। आप व्यवस्थामें बदलाव ला रहे है। मैंने आपकी प्रामाणिकता की प्रशंसा अनेक व्यक्तीयोंके माध्यमसे सुनी है। आपने ई—ऑक्शन शुरू किया। किसी भी प्रकारके राजनितीक दबावमें न आते हुये आप जो कार्य कर रहे है वह निश्चीत रूपसे सराहनीय है। घाटेमें चल रहे कोल इंडिया को मुनाफेवाली कंपनी बनानेके लिये जो कोशिश शुरू की है उसमें आप सफल हो इस हेतु मैं आपका शुभकामनाएँ देता हूँ।

आप जिस सत्यके मार्ग पर चल रहे है वह निश्चीत रूपसे काबिले तारिफ है। सत्य कभीकभी परेशान जरूर होता है लेकिन पराजित नहीं हो सकता। आपको मेरी हार्दिक शुभकामनाएँ !

आपका स्नेह एवं सहयोग सदैव अपेक्षित।

शुभकामनाओं के साथ ....

आपका स्नेहाकांक्षी

(सुधीर मुनगंटीवार)

Gaal Bazar Ward, Chandrapur (M.S.) 442 402. Tel (Off) : 07172 - 252582, (Resi) : 07172 - 256069, Fax : 07172 - 258800
Mumbai. Tel : 22021586 Extn. : 417 ■ Cell : 9822220182

Bibliography

1. Das, SK: *Civil Service Reform and Structural Adjustment*, Oxford University Press, New Delhi, India.
2. Das, SK: *Public Office, Private Interest: Bureaucracy and Corruption in India*, Oxford University Press, New Delhi, India.
3. Deshmukh, BG: *A Cabinet Secretary Looks Back: From Poona to the Prime Minister's Office*, Harper Collins, India.
4. Ghosh-Bhattacharya, Ratna: *Administration in a Developing Society*, Himalaya Publishing House, Bombay.
5. Jalan, Bimal: *The Future of India: Politics, Economics and Governance*, Penguin Books Limited.
6. John P Burns and Bidhya Bowornwathana (Eds): *Civil Service Systems in Asia*, Edward Elgar, Cheltenham, UK.
7. Kashyap, Subhash C: *The Ministers and the Legislators*, Metropolitan Book Company Limited.
8. Reddy, Sanjeev PL and Mishra, SN: *Sardar Vallabhbhai Patel: The Nation Builder*, Indian Institute of Public Administration, New Delhi.
9. Saxena, AP (Ed): *Jawaharlal Nehru and Indian Administration*, Uppal Publishing House, New Delhi.
10. Subramanian, TRS: *Journeys Through Babudom and Netaland: Governance in India*, Rupa & Co, New Delhi

Websites

1. Dr Andrew Brien (Consultant)
   A Code of Conduct for Parliamentarians (Australian Parliamentary Library Research Paper 2, 1998-99)

Politics and Public Administration Group
http://www.aph.gov.au/

2. Deirdre Mc Keown
Codes of Conduct in Australian and selected overseas Parliaments
Politics and Public Administration Section
http://www.aph.gov.au/
3. Civil Service Code
http://www.civilservice.gov.uk/
4. Ministerial Code
CABINET OFFICE
https://www.gov.uk/

Index